FROM
BOMBER COUNTY
TO BERLIN

From Bomber County to Berlin
An RAF Airman's Wartime Story

Authors: Ingrid Shepherd and Dawn Woodward

Publisher Imprint: Ingrid Shepherd and Dawn Woodward

For permissions, inquiries, or further information, please contact: ShepherdWoodwardBooks@gmail.com

ISBNs

978-1-80541-831-3 (eBook)
978-1-80541-832-0 (Paperback)

This is a work of non-fiction. All facts and events described are presented to the best of the authors' knowledge and belief.

FROM
BOMBER COUNTY
TO BERLIN

AN RAF AIRMAN'S WARTIME STORY

INGRID SHEPHERD
& DAWN WOODWARD

INTRODUCTION

From Bomber County to Berlin - An RAF Airman's WW2 Story

From Bomber County to Berlin is the true story of RAF airman Sergeant Albert Avery Walton and his crewmates, who flew with 101 Squadron during World War II. Tasked with top-secret radio jamming missions, they faced the deadliest odds in Bomber Command.

On the night of 3rd January, 1944, their Lancaster was shot down over Berlin. Albert baled out with a burning parachute, miraculously surviving by landing in a tree. Captured by German forces, he was sent to Stalag IV-B, one of the largest prisoner-of-war camps, remaining there until liberation in May 1945.

This book weaves together family memories, wartime records, and newly uncovered family accounts to bring Albert's story to life. It also honours his crewmates, each with their own journey through war, capture, and survival. Some never made it home.

From his quiet beginnings in Boldon to the perilous skies over Nazi Germany, Albert's story is one of duty, resilience, and sheer luck. From Bomber County to Berlin is a gripping tribute to the young airmen who risked everything and the bonds of brotherhood that war could never break.

Dedication

This book is dedicated to eight brave men from RAF 101 Squadron. They flew together on flight DV269 on 2nd January 1944 as part of a Bomber Command raid during World War II. On that fateful mission to Berlin, four of these courageous airmen perished and four were taken captive, becoming prisoners of war. Their sacrifice, resilience, and unwavering commitment to duty embody the spirit of a generation that risked everything for freedom.

In memory of:

- **Sergeant Albert Avery Walton** – Wireless Operator/Air Gunner
- **Sergeant Charles Lindsay** – Flight Engineer
- **Sergeant Charles 'Derek' Brown** – Special Operations Wireless Operator
- **Flight Officer Weston Craig** – Navigator
- **Flight Lieutenant Alan Lonsdale Lazenby DFC** – Pilot
- **Flight Officer James McClure** – Bomb Aimer (RCAF)
- **Sergeant Gerald Alfred Beckett** – Air Gunner (RCAF)
- **Sergeant Donald Henry (Donnie) Stephens** – Rear Gunner

May their stories be told, their memories preserved, and their sacrifices never forgotten.

Table of Contents

CHAPTER 1

The Early Years

This is the story of Albert Avery Walton, a seemingly ordinary young man from a small village whose life would take an extraordinary turn during his service in the RAF. Born into a loving family in West Boldon, County Durham (as it was then known), Albert grew up in a close-knit household where resilience, hard work, and determination were part of everyday life. The son of Alexander Walton, an Estonian national, and Caroline Mabel Tulip, a local lady, Albert's story begins with a family whose roots were anything but ordinary.

Albert's father, Alexander Walton, was born in Estonia, the youngest of seven siblings in a family steeped in the seafaring tradition. With five sisters and an older brother, Johannes, Alexander was expected to follow in his ancestors' footsteps as a merchant seaman. From an early age, Alexander worked aboard ships transporting goods between ports worldwide. However, in 1905, at the age of just nineteen, he made the bold decision to leave his homeland, stowing away on a merchant ship bound for England. He eventually arrived in South Shields, in the northeast of England.

The following text, taken from the church records in Estonia, states that Alexander Walton was originally called Aleksander Valton, his name having been anglicised for life in England.

Translated:

"Son Aleksander (Aleksander) Valton. Born 12.04.1886 in Harju village. [Emmaste parish]. Confirmed at church 02.03.1903 in Emmaste parish. According to the personal register of Emmaste parish 1905-1927, he lived in England from 1905."

Travel Document for Albert's Father

Resourceful and resilient, Alexander soon found work and lodgings despite speaking little English. By the end of the First World War, Alexander had returned to South Shields after active service in the merchant navy, surviving two torpedo attacks during the conflict. He lodged in a house at 68 Winchester Street, South Shields, run by the Tulip family, which is clearly how he met his future wife, Caroline, the daughter of the proprietors. In 1919, at the age of 33, Alexander married Caroline Mabel Tulip, who was 28, in South Shields. They quickly began building a family, welcoming their first son, Norman, in 1919, followed by Albert Avery in 1921, Elwyn in 1923, Stanley in 1926, and John Tulip in 1928. Two daughters, Anne and Hilda, completed the family in 1930 and 1933, respectively.

The Walton family lived at 10 Addison Road in West Boldon, a bustling, happy household despite the challenges of Alexander's long absences as a seaman. Caroline Mabel shouldered the responsibility of raising the children, with the older siblings helping care for the younger ones.

Albert, the second eldest, bore the name of his uncle, Albert Avery Tulip, his mother's younger brother, who had a successful career in the merchant navy and served in the RAF during World War II as a wireless operator. This connection would later mirror Albert Walton's own path, as he followed in his uncle's footsteps to become a wireless operator in the RAF.

Albert attended Boldon Intermediate School, where he excelled not only as a scholar, but also as a goalkeeper for the school's football team, leading them to victory in the 1933/34 season when they won the Cochrane Cup and the B&G Shield. His love for football continued after school, and he played for several local teams, earning accolades and trophies.

Winning the Cup! Albert is pictured centre back row;
goalkeeping was his talent!

Reverse side of post card

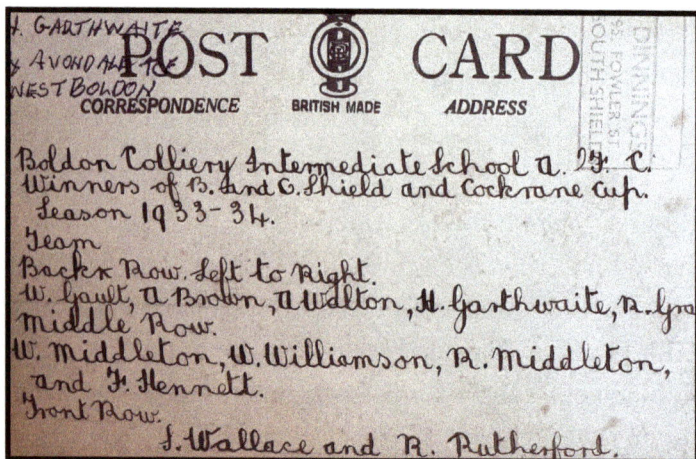

Albert (right) and older brother Norman (left) looking rather dapper.

Younger brothers Stan (left) and John (right)

On leaving school, Albert, a young man of many talents, trained as a joiner at the Bitulac Factory in Boldon, a major employer in the area. He was an active member of the local church choir and participated in social events at the Aubrey Leake Hall.

It was at one of these community dances that Albert met Lilian Chandler, the woman who would become the love of his life. Their courtship was the beginning of a bond that would endure the trials of war and separation, a testament to the strength of Albert's character and the love that defined his life.

Lilian Chandler

CHAPTER 2

War Is Declared

By March 1939, Hitler's forces had occupied the remnants of Czechoslovakia, shattering any remaining illusions that Germany's territorial ambitions could be contained. Britain and France, once hopeful that appeasement might preserve peace, now faced the grim reality that war was inevitable. Throughout the summer, newspapers were filled with ominous headlines and radio bulletins brought daily updates of diplomatic crises. Families in West Boldon, like those across the country, lived under the shadow of uncertainty, waiting for the moment when the fragile peace would finally break.

In the late summer of 1939, life in West Boldon carried on much as it always had. Albert Walton was working as a joiner at the Bitumastic company in East Boldon, spending his free time organising social events at the Aubrey Leake Hall, near St Nicholas's Church. His weekends were devoted to football, both spectating and playing; he was also a keen fisherman. To complete his happiness, Albert had a sweetheart, Lily, and life was just beginning to get interesting. Their evenings were filled with dances, laughter, and the excitement of young love, with dreams of a future together. But beneath the surface, an unspoken tension lingered; change was coming, and everyone knew it.

That moment came on Sunday, 3rd September 1939. At exactly 11:15 a.m., Prime Minister Neville Chamberlain's sombre voice crackled through the wireless sets in homes, pubs, and other public spaces across the nation. His words confirmed what many had feared but expected:

"I am speaking to you from the Cabinet Room at 10 Downing Street. This morning, the British Ambassador in Berlin handed the German Government a final note, stating that unless we heard from them by 11 o'clock that they were prepared at once to withdraw their troops from Poland, a state of war would exist between us. I have to tell you now that no such undertaking has been received and that consequently, this country is at war with Germany."

Silence followed. For a few moments, the weight of his words hung heavy in every household. Then, across the country, the reality of war set in.

Though the outbreak of war did not come as a shock, its arrival still sent ripples of fear and urgency through every town and village. In West Boldon, people braced themselves for the unknown. Almost overnight, life changed. Gas masks were issued and families practiced putting them on in their homes. Anderson shelters were hastily dug into back gardens. The government urged people to grow their own vegetables to supplement what would soon be strict wartime rations. Women learned to stretch ingredients further, making meals from whatever they could find.

For Albert and Lily, the war cast a shadow over their hopes

for the future. Would they be separated? How long would the war last? Would things ever be the same again? Like so many young couples across Britain, they faced an uncertain road ahead.

The call for volunteers rang out across the country. Some men rushed to enlist, while others joined the newly formed Local Defence Volunteers (later to become the Home Guard) or trained as Air Raid Wardens. Blackout drills were enforced, with windows covered and streetlights extinguished to make it harder for enemy bombers to target towns and cities. Scrap metal drives encouraged people to donate old pots, pans, and railings for the war effort.

Albert 1940

For now, the war was something distant, unfolding in far-off places. But the people of West Boldon knew it would not stay that way forever. A year later, in September 1940, the first waves of German bombs would begin to fall on Britain. The war, which had once seemed like something that belonged to the battlefields of Europe, would soon come to their doorstep.

2.1 "Let 'Em All Come": Albert and the Home Guard

Before Albert donned the blue uniform of the Royal Air Force, he first served closer to home as a young member of the Home Guard, a force of local volunteers formed at the outset of the Second World War to defend Britain against the looming threat of German invasion.

The Home Guard, originally called the Local Defence Volunteers (LDV), was born out of necessity in May 1940. The government issued a call to arms for all men aged 17 to 65, urging them to join their local units. It was an extraordinary display of national unity, with men from all walks of life stepping forward to do their bit for King and country. These volunteers received basic military-style training, but resources were scarce, and they were often armed with little more than clubs, pikes, and knives. Guns and ammunition were in such short supply that even homemade weapons and improvised tactics were commonplace.

Remarkably, the Home Guard welcomed boys as young as 14 and men well into their 70s, assigning them lighter duties as messengers or lookouts. These citizen soldiers were expected to give 48 hours of unpaid service per month, balancing this commitment with their regular jobs. Their task was clear: to hold the line and support the regular Army if the Nazis ever set foot on British soil.

Albert Joins the Ranks

Albert Walton was just 18 years old when he joined the

Jarrow Local Defence Volunteers Unit on 31st May 1940, signing up while still living at his family home at 10 Addison Road, West Boldon. Perhaps inspired by a sense of duty or driven by the determination to contribute to the war effort, Albert, like many young men of his time, was ready to defend his country from an uncertain and threatening future.

But Albert's time with the Home Guard was short-lived. After serving for 64 days, he was discharged on 2nd August 1940, with the note "failed to report for duty" appearing on his record. The circumstances behind this entry remain unclear. Did life at home call him away, or was it something more mundane, like a miscommunication? Or perhaps, like many young men, Albert's mind was already focused on something bigger: the desire to serve in the regular forces.

Albert's ARP Jackknife: A Rare Piece of Home Front History

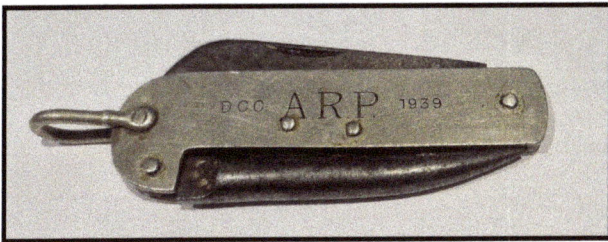

While serving on the home front in Boldon, Albert was issued a rudimentary yet practical jackknife, an essential tool for Air Raid Precautions (ARP) duties. Remarkably, this piece has been preserved within the family, a tangible link to his wartime experience and the preparations made on British soil.

The knife is a 1939 ARP jackknife manufactured by the Davenport Cutlery Company of Sheffield, a notable rarity, as most surviving examples were produced by George Gill & Sons. The knife features a single-bladed stainless-steel body, a marlin spike, and a lanyard ring for easy carrying. Both the blade and spike show signs of use, with the blade lightly patinated and spike sharpened at the tip, yet it remains in good overall condition and fully functional.

Stamped clearly with "Sheffield, England" at the base of the blade, this pattern of jackknife was produced for a limited time and ceased manufacture in 1939, adding to its rarity. Tools like this would have been vital for a range of ARP tasks such as cutting through debris, assisting in rescues, and performing general utility work during air raids.

Holding this knife today offers a direct connection to Albert's wartime reality, a symbol of resilience, preparedness, and the practical tools that supported both frontline and home front efforts during Britain's darkest hours.

A Stepping Stone to Greater Things

Whatever the reason for his departure from the Home Guard, this brief chapter of Albert's life offers a glimpse into his early commitment to defending his country. From guarding the home front to eventually soaring the skies with the RAF, the young man from West Boldon had already shown a willingness to step forward when Britain needed him most.

Local Defence Volunteer Form 1940

B.

ORM OF ENROLMENT IN THE LOCAL DEFENCE VOLUNTEERS.

Name **WALTON** Christian Names **ALBERT AVERY**

Surname in Block Letters.

Questions to be put on Enrolment.

1. Albert Avery Walton
2. 19. 27 May 1921.
3. 10 Addison Rd. W. Borden
4. (a) Yes   Restrictions removed.
   (b) Father. # Bohemian.   (Flier Approval)
   Mother. British.
   (c) Mabel Walton (mother)
       10 Addison Rd.
       W. Borden
5. no
6. Yes
7. Yes
8. Yes   Service no longer
9. Yes   required

DECLARATION.

I, Albert Avery Walton de solemnly declare that the answers made by me to the foregoing questions are true and I hereby agree to serve in the Local Defence Volunteers.

Signature of applicant   A A Walton

Date May 31/40   Signature of enrolling authority   Ernest Fox Jun

CERTIFICATE OF ACCEPTANCE.

...A. A. Walton...(name) is accepted for service in the Local Defence Volunteers for the following period

(a) the duration of the emergency.

or (b) until ...

Date....31/5/40.   Signature of accepting authority.

13

31/5/40

Total service towards engagement in the Home Guard to...2/9/42...
(date of discharge) ....years ..64.....days.

Discharged on (date)...2/9/42....in consequence of ....
..............Failed to report for duty........................

The discharge of the above named is hereby confirmed.

Station..........East Kirkby..........

Date ....24/11/.......19 41

Signature.................................
(To be completed by official
competent to confirm discharge)

Insert cause of discharge, quoting authority.

CHAPTER 3

Early Days in the RAF

On the 16th of April 1941, Albert Avery Walton began his journey into the Royal Air Force (RAF), aged just nineteen years old. Like so many of his generation, he stepped forward in the nation's hour of need, leaving behind his family home in Boldon to enlist as a Wireless Operator/Air Gunner. Albert's first destination was RAF Padgate Recruitment Centre, a bustling non-flying RAF station in Lancashire. Padgate served as the gateway for countless young recruits during the Second World War; it was responsible for basic training, interviews and, assigning personnel to specialist courses.

It was at Padgate (No.3 Recruitment Centre) that Albert's military journey began in earnest. Recruits, fresh-faced and eager, were introduced to military life and discipline, including parade drills, basic physical training, and rudimentary instruction on RAF operations.

During training, recruits were housed in wooden barracks designed to accommodate twenty individuals. Each barrack featured two rows of beds, each paired with a locker, and a separate room at one end for the corporal drill instructor. Heating was provided by two coke stoves, ensuring warmth during colder periods. A separate hut at the rear contained the washing facilities.

Maintaining impeccable personal kit was a fundamental aspect of training. Recruits were required to Blanco and polish their equipment to meet the exacting standards of the non-commissioned officers and, ultimately, the officers. Detailed diagrams specified the precise layout and folding methods for kit inspections, with everything needing to be in its designated place. Achieving this level of precision demanded days of diligent effort to pass the rigorous inspections.

These practices instilled self-discipline and pride in appearance, essential qualities for service members. Regular inspections ensured that all equipment was present and correctly maintained, fostering a sense of order and responsibility among the recruits.

Many of the men, like Albert, would soon be earmarked for vital aircrew roles. The process was rigorous, sorting the wheat from the chaff for the demanding positions that lay ahead. For Albert, this marked the first step in what would become an extraordinary story of courage and resilience.

Wireless Training: Learning the Art of Communication

Training to become a Wireless Operator in the RAF was an intense and demanding process. Days began early, with classes running six days a week from 8 a.m. to 6 p.m. The trainees were immersed in both the theory and practical operation of radio communications and studied the mechanics and maintenance of various wireless sets, including the Marconi R1155 receiver and T1154 transmitter. Both sets were vital equipment for bomber crews.

A significant portion of their training took place in classrooms, where mastering Morse Code was a top priority. Trainees were required to both send and receive messages with increasing speed and accuracy. To develop proficiency, a structured system was used. Students started at a beginner level, with the aim to send and receive Morse Code at six words per minute. Once they met the required standard, they moved on to a more advanced level, where speeds of eight words per minute were expected. The progression continued until they reached the target of twelve words per minute, the minimum standard for operational duty.

The training environment was competitive, with students pushing each other to improve their skills. The ability to send and interpret Morse Code under pressure was essential; lives would depend on it in combat situations. In addition to radio communication, Wireless Operators were also trained in alternative signalling methods. If their radio equipment failed, they needed to rely on the Aldis signalling lamp to send visual Morse Code messages.

Once they had passed the course, their role would be critical in coordinating missions, relaying vital messages, and ensuring the crew remained connected with command, even in the chaos of battle.

Wireless Operators also undertook a six-week course at the Air Gunnery School. They learned to operate the turrets and guns, as they could be called upon to operate any of the gun positions within a Lancaster Bomber.

A Token of Love – The Sweetheart Ring

Albert was heartbroken leaving Lily behind to begin his RAF training. The two were inseparable, their bond was unshakable, and the thought of parting was almost unbearable. Like so many young couples at the time, the war would force them into separate lives with miles of uncertainty stretching between them.

Wanting to give Lily something to hold onto while they were apart, Albert decided to buy her a sweetheart ring, a symbol of his love and devotion. He had found the perfect ring at Harris's The Jewellers, a well-known shop in Pink Lane, Newcastle. This historic street, one of the oldest parts of the city, was conveniently located near Newcastle Central Station, where he had previously departed on his journey.

The Sweetheart Ring

The ring was a delicate gold heart, set with three tiny stones: a diamond, a sapphire, and a ruby. It wasn't extravagant, but its meaning was priceless. As they faced months of separation, hardship, and uncertainty, the ring became a cherished reminder that, no matter the distance, they belonged to each other.

By 18th November, 1941, Albert's RAF record card made note of his skill and potential, describing him as an "Excellent Wireless Operator," a commendation that highlighted both his technical abilities and his dedication to his training. His proficiency would be crucial in the coming years, ensuring seamless communication during dangerous bombing missions. The RAF's training program, already a well-oiled machine by this stage of the war, was relentless. Airmen were constantly pushed to their limits to prepare for the unforgiving realities of combat.

In 1942, it was decided that aircrew training had to undergo a comprehensive reorganisation. In future, those who passed a formalised selection process would be considered full-time professional aircrew. They would be given a demanding and expensive training programme, and, when qualified, they would be awarded a new style of one-winged brevet according to their crew role. They would then be paid a generous flying pay allowance above their normal pay. They were immediately commissioned or promoted to a new rank of Sergeant (aircrew).

Albert's RAF career saw steady progress, reflected in a series of promotions as he moved through the various schools and ranks:

- Aircraftman (AC)
- Aircraftman Second Class (2AC)
- Sergeant (Sgt) — promoted on 9th April 1943, marking a significant milestone in his service

Training for War (1943)

From Ansons to Lancasters: The Path to Bomber Command

The pages of Sgt Albert Walton's flight log book offer a vivid record of his transformation from trainee to fully operational airman. His 1943 training saw him progress through multiple aircraft types, each stage building the specialist skills he would need as a Wireless Operator on heavy bomber raids over enemy territory.

April–June 1943: Core Training in the Avro Anson

Albert began flying in the Avro Anson, a twin-engine air-craft originally introduced in the 1930s for maritime reconnaissance but later widely used by the RAF as a training aircraft. Its forgiving handling and stable flight characteristics made it ideal for training wireless operators, navigators, and bomb aimers.

During these months, Albert's log shows a multitude of short flights with various pilots — a sign of a foundational training phase where crews rotated frequently to build basic aircrew skills. The Anson's typical cruising speed of around 120–140 mph, along with its onboard wireless and navigation equipment, gave Albert the chance to practice real-time communication, code transmission, and intercom procedures under flight conditions.

July 1943: Meeting F/O Lazenby – and the Whitley V

On 15 July 1943, a significant name appears in the log book: F/O Lazenby, the pilot who would become Albert's crew commander throughout their operational tour. The second half of July saw them flying together regularly in the Armstrong Whitworth Whitley Mark V, a long-range twin-engine bomber that by 1943 had been retired from front-line service but remained in use for Operational Training Units (OTUs).

Outdated and affectionately dubbed "The Flying Coffin" due to its awkward nose-down flying attitude, even when in level flight, the aircraft's nose appeared to be pointing downward, relative to the horizon.

Even so the Whitley still gave new crews valuable experience in navigation, formation flying, and especially bombing techniques. Much of their time together that month was spent mastering bombing runs — a complex team process requiring precise coordination between bomb aimer, pilot, navigator, and wireless operator.

10th August 1943: The Heavy Conversion Unit – Halifax Bombers

Albert's next step took him to No. 1667 Heavy Conversion Unit (HCU) at RAF Faldingworth, where he began flying in Handley Page Halifax bombers. This four-engine heavy bomber, powered by Rolls-Royce Merlin or Bristol Hercules engines depending on the mark, was one of the RAF's principal strategic bombers, sharing much of the front-line burden with the Avro Lancaster.

The Halifax was more physically demanding for crews — larger, heavier, and louder than anything Albert had flown before. It could carry up to 13,000 lbs of bombs and had a crew of seven. At the HCU, Albert flew with F/O Lawrence, F/O Mohardy, and of course F/O Lazenby, honing essential skills for operational readiness.

Remarks in the log book during this period show an intense programme of advanced exercises:

- Bombing practice – with real bomb runs over training ranges.
- Cross-country flights – long-range navigation under various conditions, often at night.
- 'Bullseye' exercises – large-scale mock bombing raids designed to simulate the chaos and complexity of real operations.
- Fighter affiliation – defensive manoeuvres against fighter aircraft, often with Spitfires or Hurricanes acting as mock attackers.

IR (likely Infra-Red or Identification Recognition) – may refer to formation flying and coordination under blackout conditions or with minimal lighting.

September 1943: The Final Transition – Flying the Lancaster I

From 14 September 1943, Albert and F/O Lazenby were joined by F/O James McClure, a Bomb Aimer from R.C.A.F. according to McClure's flight log book. The three participated in numerous training flights together throughout the month, almost exclusively flying the Avro

Lancaster Mark I, the most celebrated of all RAF bombers. With four Rolls-Royce Merlin engines, a top speed of over 280 mph, and a maximum bomb load of 22,000 lbs, the Lancaster was a formidable machine — fast, agile for its size, and essential to the RAF's strategic bombing campaign.

Now a cohesive crew, Walton and Lazenby's training flights in the Lancaster reflected increasing complexity and pressure. Everything they'd learned — communication, navigation, formation flying, evasive action, and bombing — had to come together. The log book entries reveal that they were ready. Soon, they would be posted to No. 101 Squadron, and face the reality of war.

3.1   A Wartime Wedding – Albert & Lily's Marriage

By this point in in his training, Albert was a married man. A year earlier, the 27th of June, 1942, was one of the most significant days in Albert's life — the day he married his darling Lily.

An account of that day follows:

In the hours leading up to the ceremony, the two households were filled with a mix of excitement and emotion. Lily prepared at her family home at 207 Charles Street, Boldon Colliery, surrounded by her mother, Maud Chandler, and her siblings. Her father had sadly passed away when she was a child, as had her sister Maud and her brother Alfred. Meanwhile, Albert's family gathered at 10 Addison Road,

West Boldon, preparing for the momentous occasion. As the first of his siblings to marry, Albert's wedding was a cause for great excitement in the Walton household.

Lily, a skilled dressmaker, crafted her own wedding gown with care and precision, ensuring she looked as beautiful as ever despite wartime fabric shortages. Albert, standing proudly in his RAF airman's dress uniform, looked smart and dashing, ready to embark on a new chapter of life with his sweetheart.

Wedding Day Photo

Family Photo

Like many young couples during wartime, there was an urgency to marry before Albert was sent into active service. For some, marriage was a way to cement their bond before inevitable separation, offering a sense of security in uncertain times. There was also a practical reason: aircrew survival rates were frighteningly low. Forty-four percent were killed and just twenty-four percent made it through the war unscathed and uncaptured. If the worst were to happen, wives would receive a widow's allowance, ensuring financial support. But for Albert and Lily, this was more than a wartime necessity; it was a promise of a future together, no matter what lay ahead.

The couple exchanged their vows at St Nicholas's Church, West Boldon; a place rich with memories for Albert, who had once sung in its choir. The reception followed at The Aubrey Leake Hall, a fitting location where Albert had helped organise dances and social events in happier times. But today, the hall wasn't hosting a community gathering: it was celebrating an extraordinary union.

With wartime rationing in full force, the wedding feast would have been a simple affair, but no less special. Friends, family, and even neighbours all chipped in, donating precious rations to help provide a meal for the celebration. The wedding cake, traditionally the centrepiece of any reception, would have been a wartime compromise, a clever mix of whatever ingredients could be spared, with at least one tier possibly being a cardboard replica to maintain appearances.

Though wartime meant some loved ones were absent, including family members serving in the forces, Richard ("Dicky") Chandler, Lily's younger brother, and T. Foster stood as witnesses. Despite the challenges ahead, Albert and Lily's love was unwavering. Theirs was a marriage that would face separation, war, and hardship, not to mention bring countless moments of joy in the years to come.

After a brief period of wedding leave, Albert had to return to his RAF training base, now a married man. For Lily, saying goodbye so soon after their wedding was heartbreaking, but she held onto the hope that, one day, the war would end, and they would finally be together for good.

Lily's Lucky Christmas Pudding

Later that year, Lily and Albert enjoyed their first Christmas together as a married couple. Lily was a fantastic cook, but she truly excelled in baking. From the moment Albert first tasted her apple pies, he knew he was on to something good. The Christmas after their wedding, Albert was granted leave, a precious opportunity to return home and spend time with his new wife and family.

Determined to make it a Christmas to remember, Lily spent weeks preparing, carefully collecting ingredients and saving ration tickets. The highlight of the meal would be her Christmas pudding, made with her own secret recipe: dried fruit soaked in sweet tea with a splash of brandy for extra richness.

As tradition dictated, she wrapped a silver thrupenny bit in greaseproof paper and buried it deep in the pudding mixture before steaming it for hours until it was perfectly cooked. Finding the hidden coin was said to bring good luck, an ancient superstition that Lily was keen to uphold.

On Christmas Day, she proudly served up the pudding, making sure Albert received the slice containing the lucky 1919 thrupenny. He carried it with him on all his missions, tucked safely in his pocket as a talisman. Through all the dangers he faced in the skies, the tiny silver coin remained with him, a token of love, tradition, and a little extra luck.

CHAPTER 4

Joining 101 Squadron

U pon completing his training at Faldingworth, Albert was released to join 101 Squadron, one of the most prestigious units within Bomber Command. The squadron was located in Lincolnshire, the county which earned the nickname "Bomber County" during World War II due to its significant role in RAF Bomber Command operations. The county hosted nearly seventy air bases, more than any other in England, making it a central hub for bomber operations. This extensive network of airfields contributed to its enduring association with bomber aviation.

By this stage, the Lancaster bomber had become the backbone of the RAF's night-bombing operations and 101 Squadron was at the cutting edge of the campaign. Albert's transfer to 101 Squadron represented the culmination of over two years of arduous preparation. For him, the journey from being a fresh recruit at Padgate to a Sergeant in Bomber Command was one of dedication, determination, and the steadfast resolve of a young man ready to serve his country.

Wireless Operator/Air Gunner (WAG) – Role and Responsibilities

The Wireless Operator/Air Gunner (WAG) played a dual role aboard RAF bombers during World War II. Primarily responsible for radio communications, the Wireless Operator maintained contact with ground stations, received navigation updates, and assisted the Observer (Navigator) in determining positional fixes through triangulation. This was critical for course corrections, particularly during long-range night operations.

In addition to communication duties, the Wireless Operator was also a trained Air Gunner, responsible for manning one of the aircraft's defensive machine guns when under attack. Positioned at a designated gun station, often in the mid-upper or ventral position, the WAG was tasked with engaging enemy aircraft, relaying threats to the crew, and providing suppressive fire to increase the bomber's chances of survival.

A fully qualified Wireless Operator/Air Gunner held the rank of Sergeant and wore a single-wing aircrew brevet with a wreath encircling the letters "WAG" above his left breast pocket. On the right arm, a cloth patch featuring a lightning bolt symbol denoted the trade specialisation. The role required extensive training in both radio operations and aerial gunnery, ensuring that WAGs could perform under the extreme conditions of combat.

4.1   A Legend of the Skies

The Avro Lancaster, affectionately nicknamed "The Lanc", was the workhorse of RAF Bomber Command during the Second World War. Designed and manufactured by Avro, it was a four-engine heavy bomber powered by Rolls-Royce

Merlin engines, the same engines that propelled the iconic Spitfire fighter. Introduced into service in 1942, the Lancaster became synonymous with the night bombing raids that targeted industrial and military infrastructure deep within Nazi-occupied Europe.

The "Lanc."

With its sleek yet imposing design, the Lancaster was not known for its speed but for its remarkable payload capacity and versatility. Its 33 foot long, unobstructed bomb bay allowed it to carry the largest bombs in the RAF arsenal, including the 4,000 lb (1,800 kg) "Cookie," the 8,000 lb (3,600 kg) "Super Cookie," the massive 12,000 lb (5,400 kg) "Tallboy," and 22,000 lb (10,000 kg) "Grand Slam." These bombs, combined with a substantial load of smaller incendiaries, made the Lancaster a devastating weapon against enemy infrastructure.

More than just a delivery vehicle for destruction, the Lancaster demonstrated its versatility in some of the war's most daring operations. It was the aircraft chosen to equip the legendary 617 Squadron for Operation Chastise, better known as the Dambusters Raid. Modified to carry Barnes Wallis's innovative bouncing bomb, the Lancaster played a key role in the destruction of Germany's Ruhr Valley dams, disrupting water supplies and industrial production.

By the end of the war, the Lancaster had undertaken more than 150,000 sorties, solidifying its place as the backbone of RAF Bomber Command. Crewed by men from across the Commonwealth and occupied Europe, it was a symbol of international cooperation against tyranny. Though slow and vulnerable to enemy fighters, its robust design and reliable performance made it a favourite among aircrews. For many, the Lancaster became more than an aircraft: it was a lifeline in the unforgiving skies over Europe.

Although 7,377 Lancaster Bombers were made between 1941 and 1946, half were destroyed in battle and only two remain airworthy today, one at the Battle of Britain Memorial Flight (BBMF) and the other at the Canadian Warplane Heritage Museum (CWHM).

4.2   Wings Across the Waters: The Canadian Lancasters

As war raged across Europe, the British and their Allies faced the immense challenge of producing enough aircraft to sustain the fight. To minimise the risk of enemy attacks on vital manufacturing facilities, Britain looked beyond its own borders and turned to Canada, a nation with vast resources and a growing industrial base. In a remarkably short time, Canadian factories were producing thousands of aircraft, ranging from trainers to frontline combat planes. But perhaps their most significant contribution was the production of the legendary Lancaster bomber.

Building a Lancaster in Canada

On 18th September, 1941, Britain made the pivotal decision to manufacture Lancasters in Canada. The first design blueprints arrived in January 1942, marking the start of an ambitious project for a country still emerging from the Great Depression. The scale of the task was staggering; each Lancaster required 500,000 manufacturing operations and was composed of 55,000 individual parts. Even with engines and turrets counted as single components, the complexity of production was immense.

To guide this effort, a Lancaster (R5727) was flown across the Atlantic in August 1942 to serve as a pattern aircraft. The Canadian government soon established Victory Aircraft Ltd. in Malton, Ontario, to oversee production. Every major component had to match its British counterpart to ensure that damaged aircraft could be repaired using standard parts regardless of origin.

The engines, though the same Rolls-Royce Merlin design, were built under license by Packard in the United States. Meanwhile, instruments and radio equipment were sourced from Canadian and American manufacturers. Initially, all major components were built in Malton, except for bomb doors, flaps, ailerons, and elevators, which were produced by Ottawa Car & Aircraft Ltd. As production expanded, additional subcontractors contributed: Canadian General Electric Co. Ltd. in Toronto built fuel tanks, tailplanes, fins and rudders, while Fleet Aircraft Limited in Fort Erie, Ontario, manufactured outer wings.

From blueprint to first test flight, the Canadian Lancaster program took just sixteen months, an extraordinary achievement. The workforce, many of whom were women and previously unskilled labourers, swelled from 3,300 in 1942 to 9,521 in 1944.

The Ruhr Express and Canada's Wartime Effort

The first Canadian-built Lancaster, KB700, rolled off the production line on 1st August, 1943, and was christened the Ruhr Express. The aircraft's completion was a source of immense national pride and, when it arrived in England, it was met with high praise. The chief inspector at A.V. Roe, the company behind the Lancaster's original design, remarked, "That's how an airplane should be built."

At its peak, Victory Aircraft Ltd. was producing one Lancaster per day, with a total of 430 Lancaster Mk X bombers built. Most were assigned to No. 6 Group, the Royal Canadian Air Force's (RCAF) dedicated component of Bomber Command, solidifying Canada's all-in commitment to the war effort.

The Canadian-built Lancasters performed admirably in combat. Approximately 100 were lost during wartime service, with 70 missing in action and 30 crashing on return from missions or during training. The most storied of these aircraft, KB732, completed 83 successful operations with 419 Squadron, more than any other Canadian Lancaster.

Tragically, the Ruhr Express met a premature end on 2nd January, 1945, following a mission to Nuremberg. While attempting to land, the aircraft experienced hydraulic failure, overshot the runway and crashed into a farmer's field, where it collided with a trench digger. The crew escaped amid exploding ammunition, but the bomber was consumed by fire. The loss was particularly heartbreaking because plans had been in place to return KB700 to Canada after its 50th mission as a national war memorial.

Postwar Legacy: Lancaster Variants and Civilian Use

With the war in Europe ending in May 1945, Canadian Lancaster squadrons played a vital role in repatriating former prisoners of war, many of them fellow airmen. The bombers were then flown back to Canada in preparation for deployment to the Pacific as part of "Tiger Force," a planned Commonwealth air offensive against Japan. However, the atomic bombings of Hiroshima and Nagasaki brought the war to a sudden end and the Lancasters' mission was cancelled.

Back home, the iconic bombers made one final dramatic display. In the Autumn of 1945, Canadian aircrews, overjoyed at surviving the war, flew their Lancasters at treetop level over prairie towns, buzzing farms and scaring livestock before landing their aircraft for the last time. With the war over, the government faced the question of what to do with the fleet. Many Lancasters were sold to farmers for a few hundred dollars, their parts repurposed for agricultural use: tailwheels on threshing machines, bomb-bay doors as garden borders, and escape hatches as outhouse windows.

Meanwhile, others were modified for peacetime roles. Fourteen Lancasters were converted for aerial reconnaissance and mapped the vast northern reaches of Canada, a role they performed until 1962. Another 70 aircraft were adapted for maritime patrol and served throughout the Cold War in anti-submarine roles. These conversions involved the removal of gun turrets, installation of sonobuoy systems, and even the addition of a small kitchen stove for long patrols.

In addition to its military contributions, the Lancaster also helped usher in the era of transatlantic air travel. Eight Canadian-built Lancasters were converted into long-range passenger transports, known as Lancaster XPPs (Passenger Planes). These aircraft, operated under the Canadian Government Trans-Atlantic Air Service (CGTAS) until 1947 and reduced crossing times to just over thirteen hours. This service later evolved into Trans Canada Air Lines, the forerunner of Air Canada.

A Lasting Canadian Impact

Although Victory Aircraft Ltd. produced only one example of the Avro Lincoln, a larger successor to the Lancaster and a single Avro York transport aircraft, the experience gained during the Lancaster program played a crucial role in shaping Canada's aerospace industry. Malton's facility later became Avro Canada, the company behind the legendary Avro Arrow jet interceptor.

The Lancaster's postwar story included one final Canadian connection: TW870, a British-built Lancaster that was abandoned in Newfoundland after a landing accident in 1946. Instead of being scrapped, it was purchased by Canadian entrepreneurs, converted into a fuel tanker, and operated commercially until it crashed in 1953—an unlikely second life for a machine designed for war.

Canada's role in producing the Lancaster was a defining chapter in its wartime history. From the assembly lines of Malton to the skies over Europe, these bombers and the men and women who built and flew them made a profound impact on the war effort. Though many were lost in combat, repurposed, or scrapped, their legacy endures in the few surviving examples displayed in museums across the country. The Canadian-built Lancaster remains a symbol of resilience, ingenuity, and the nation's vital contribution to the Allied victory.

4.3 Inside an RAF Bomber Crew: Roles and Responsibilities

During World War II, an RAF bomber crew operated as a unified team, with each member playing a crucial, specialised role. Their collective aim was to navigate to the target, deliver their payload, and return safely—no small feat given the dangers of every mission. Strong bonds formed through shared hardships, as each man's life depended on the others.

Prior to 1942, bomber crews were smaller, with many performing dual roles, such as navigators doubling as bomb-aimers and wireless operators serving as air gunners. However, with the introduction of larger, heavier bombers, crews expanded to seven members, allowing for more specialised positions. In the case of 101 Squadron, the crew had an additional 8th man.

Crew Positions Within an Avro Lancaster WWII Heavy Bomber

Pilot (Captain of the Aircraft)

The pilot held overall command and was responsible for flying the aircraft and managing the crew. Rank was irrelevant once in the air; the pilot's authority was absolute. In emergencies, his duty was to remain at the controls until the crew had evacuated, often putting his life at greater risk to give others a chance to survive.

Bomb Aimer

Introduced in 1942 with the arrival of seven-man heavy

bomber crews, the bomb aimer played a crucial role in ensuring the success of each operation. Positioned in the nose of the aircraft, he was responsible for guiding the pilot during the bombing run, lying flat to get a clear view of the target. Using a bombsight, a precise optical device, he calculated the correct release point by factoring in altitude, speed, direction, and atmospheric conditions.

As the aircraft approached its objective, the bomb aimer directed the pilot's course adjustments until the target was in position. In the seconds after the bombs were released, a photograph was taken as proof of the attack and for intelligence purposes, allowing the crew to count the mission toward their total operations.

In addition to his primary role, the bomb aimer received some flight training and could act as a reserve pilot in an emergency. His ability to take over the controls added an extra layer of security in the event of an incapacitated pilot.

Navigator

Ensuring the bomber stayed on course fell to the navigator, who guided the crew to their target and back, often under immense pressure and for flights lasting up to seven hours. Before the crew structure expanded, navigators also acted as bomb-aimers; however, with newer bombers, this became a distinct role.

Flight Engineer (Role added with heavy bombers in 1942)

The flight engineer oversaw the aircraft's complex mechanical systems, including fuel management, hydraulics, and electrics. Working closely with the pilot, especially during take-off and landing, he also calculated fuel usage and could step in as a backup bomb aimer. On the ground, he coordinated with maintenance crews to keep the aircraft mission ready.

Wireless Operator

Communications with base and other aircraft were the wireless operator's responsibility. Although many missions required radio silence, his role was vital during emergencies to send distress signals or positional updates and listen out for beacons that gave a steady signal tone if the pilot was on the correct line of approach to the aerodrome; too far to port, he would hear a series of Morse dots, too far to starboard, a series of dashes. He also served as a backup gunner and attended to technical faults within the aircraft. If the aircraft had to ditch into the sea, he had to remain at his post to send out a distress signal to improve the crew's chance of being located and rescued.

Air Gunners (Mid-Upper and Rear Turrets)

Stationed apart from the main crew, the mid-upper and rear gunners spent entire missions in cramped, exposed turrets, constantly scanning for enemy fighters. Their vigilance and quick reactions were essential to defending the bomber from aerial attacks. Conditions were so cold, each gunner had an electrically heated flight suit to prevent frostbite.

Special Operations Wireless Operator (Exclusive to 101 Squadron)

101 Squadron carried an additional crew member trained in the German language to operate the Airborne Cigar (ABC) jamming system. By disrupting enemy communications, they significantly hindered German night-fighter coordination. This vital but dangerous role made their aircraft prime targets for enemy interception.

Each crew member's contribution was essential. Survival depended on teamwork, trust, and the ability to perform under extraordinary pressure—qualities that defined every mission flown over hostile territory.

CHAPTER 5

Lilian on the Home Front

B ack in Boldon Colliery, Albert's wife, Lilian, was also playing her part in the war effort. Having spent some years working as a seamstress at Murray Tailors in East Boldon where she became proficient in sewing, Lilian was always smartly dressed. Murray Tailors were extremely busy making uniforms, as was almost every tailor in the country.

In support of her darling husband, she's pictured here wearing her RAF sweetheart brooch on an outfit that looks very like a uniform. Around this time, Lilian had upped her involvement in the war effort and started working in what she referred to as a munitions factory. It is unclear at which site she was located: initially it seemed that it was the local Anti-Aircraft Supply Unit in East Boldon. However, as she used to tell family that her job was to 'make bombs,' it's unlikely that she worked at this site in Boldon; more probably, she would have attended one of the other works, such as that in Birtley or Jarrow.

Lilian

She worked tirelessly at the ammunition and bomb assembly line, a vital yet dangerous role that required precision and dedication. Factories like this one were critical to Britain's war effort, as they produced munitions used by Allied forces in Europe and beyond. The work was hazardous, with a constant risk of explosions, and employees like Lilian often worked long hours under immense pressure. Her contribution to the war effort reflected the strength and determination of the women on the home front who kept the wheels of industry turning while their loved ones served abroad.

Sweetheart Brooch as seen worn above

5.1   Lest We Forget: Private Harold Chandler

Happiness was interspersed with great sadness as Lilian's brother, Albert's brother-in-law, Harold, who served in the Durham Light Infantry, was killed in action in March 1943 in Tunisia. His name is inscribed at the Medjez-el-Bab War Memorial in Tunisia.

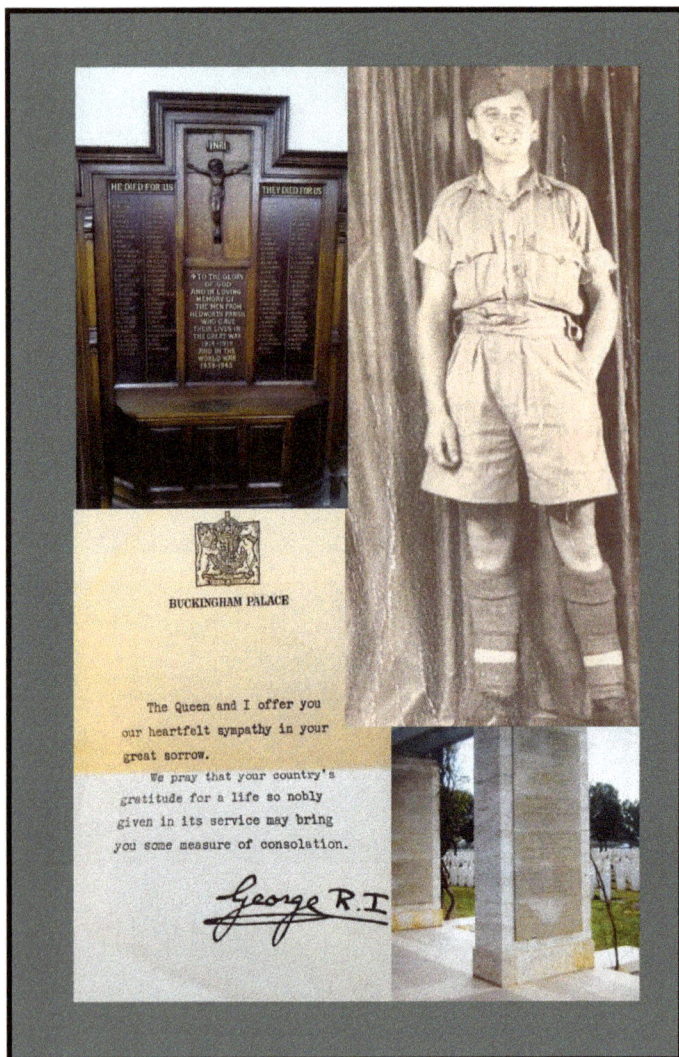

Harold, along with other local men, is also remembered at St Nicholas's Church, Boldon Colliery, where his name is inscribed into a copper plate mounted on a wooden memorial near the altar.

5.2 Lest We Forget: Able Seaman Norman Walton

The Walton family endured unspeakable loss during the war and, for Albert, the tragedy of his elder brother's death at sea must have weighed heavily on his mind throughout his own service. Able Seaman Norman Walton (P/JX 282301) served aboard the destroyer HMS Beverley, a vital yet vulnerable escort ship protecting convoys in the perilous waters of the North Atlantic.

Albert (right) and Norman (left)

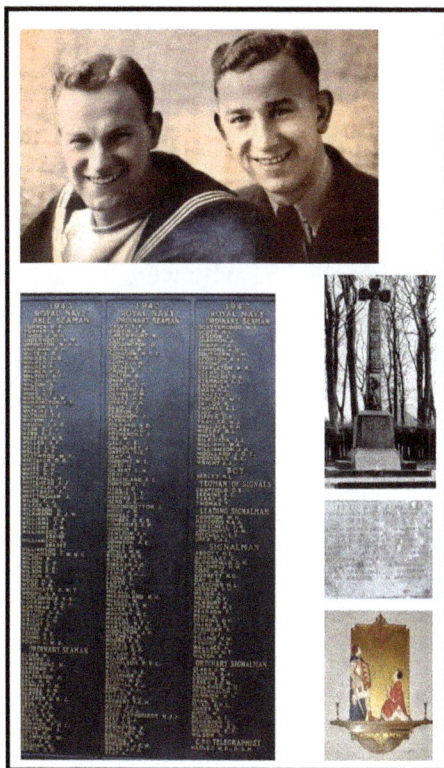

On the night of 9th April, 1943, disaster struck when HMS Beverley collided with the British steam merchant vessel Cairnvalona and sustained significant damage. The Cairnvalona had been built in Sunderland in 1918, a port very close to Norman's own home. Despite her valiant efforts to continue her mission, the collision left HMS Beverley compromised and lagging at the rear of Convoy ON-176, southwest of Iceland, in a dangerous position that made her an easy target.

Just 30 hours later, in the early hours of 11th April, 1943, Beverley fell victim to the relentless German submarine U-118. At 05:49, the U-boat fired its torpedoes, and HMS Beverley was struck. The destroyer, already struggling to stay afloat, succumbed to the icy waters of the Atlantic, her fate sealed.

Of the 155 men aboard, only four survived. Norman Walton was among the 151 who were lost at sea that fateful morning. He was just twenty-four years old. His body was never recovered, and his sacrifice is commemorated on the Portsmouth Naval Memorial, where his name is inscribed on panel 76, a silent tribute to his courage. He is also remembered locally on the East Boldon War Memorial, where his name stands alongside those of others who gave their lives.

Inside St Nicholas's Church in West Boldon, a beautiful and moving memorial plaque honours two young men from the parish who died in service during the Second World War—Norman Walton, Royal Navy, and Gordon

Egerton, an Air Raid Precautions (ARP) warden. The plaque features half-relief plaster figures of St Timothy and St Stephen gazing upward toward a gilded cross, symbolising faith and sacrifice. Beneath the figures, a brass inscription reads: "In memory of faithful servers Gordon Egerton ARP and Norman Walton RN who gave their lives on duty for their country. Placed here in 1946 by their fellow worshippers in grateful affection. R.I.P." Installed by members of the congregation shortly after the war, the plaque stands as a heartfelt tribute to the courage and devotion of two young men who served their community and country with quiet dignity.

A Brother's Loss

For Albert, serving in the skies above Europe, the news of Norman's death must have been devastating. Norman had been his older brother, a steady presence in his life, and now he was gone, claimed by the unforgiving North Atlantic. The thought of Norman's final moments aboard a sinking ship in the icy waters may have haunted Albert during his own dangerous missions.

The Walton family's grief was shared by many across the nation, as countless families bore similar losses during the war. Yet for Albert, the shadow of Norman's sacrifice may have given him an even greater determination to carry on, to serve his country and to do his duty, just as Norman had.

For Albert's mother, Caroline, and the rest of the family, this blow was devastating. Norman's younger sister Anne recalled, "It was Easter time, I'd been out with my mother (Caroline), and we'd had a really lovely day. I remember my mother saying it would be a 'perfect' day if a letter arrived from Norman… the next day a letter did arrive, to say he was lost at sea."

CHAPTER 6

1943: Fully Qualified and Ready for Action!

Now proudly sporting a host of new badges to mark his achievements as promotions:

- Sergeant Stripes to left arm
- AG Winged Brevet left Chest
- RAF Albatross patches right and left shoulder
- Wireless Operator's 'Sparks' trade patch to right shoulder (not visible on this photo)

Lily must have treasured this last photo taken together before Albert started his operational service in 101 Squadron.

"Mens Agitat Molem" - Mind Over Matter

In Autumn, 1943, Sergeant Albert Avery Walton stepped into the world of 101 Squadron at Ludford Magna, near Market Rasen, Lincs.. At 22 years old, he was now a fully trained Wireless Operator, receiving a handsome pay rise. He was earning nine shillings a day, more than doubling his previous wage. Just weeks earlier, he had completed his RAF training with flying colours. Yet nothing could have fully prepared him for what awaited in this groundbreaking, highly classified unit.

Albert's 101 Squadron Badge

101 Squadron was no ordinary group within Bomber Command. While it had a fleet of over 40 Lancaster Bombers, 200 ground staff, and over 300 aircrew, it was at the forefront of a revolutionary and top-secret initiative: Airborne Cigar, or ABC. This cutting-edge, highly classified system was designed to disrupt German air defences by jamming their radio communications. Every Lancaster bomber in this squadron was retrofitted with 600 pounds of specialised radio equipment, invisible to most except for the telltale presence of three long external antennae, one of which, resembling a cigar, gave the project its name.

Whether Albert knew the full scope of the work he was about to undertake when he arrived at Ludford Magna is unclear. But what is certain is that this was no ordinary posting. Each Lancaster within this 'Secret Squadron' now carried an additional eighth crew member, a Special Operations Wireless Operator who spoke German and who had a crucial role in the nightly bombing raids over Europe. These operators were tasked with tuning into German radio communications, identifying enemy frequencies, and transmitting loud tones to block messages between German fighter pilots and their ground controllers. This work disrupted the Luftwaffe's coordination and gave Allied bombers a fighting chance in the skies.

The weight of this extra equipment, combined with the additional crew member, meant that 101 Squadron's Lancasters carried a slightly reduced bomb load. Yet their contributions to the war effort were immeasurable. Two of these ABC-equipped aircraft would accompany larger formations on sorties, jamming enemy signals and shielding their comrades from coordinated attacks while participating in bombing missions themselves.

Their missions were so critical to the Allied effort that, while on the ground, 101's aircraft were placed under 24-hour armed guard. The secrecy surrounding ABC meant that even the men on the ground often had no idea what the eighth crew member's role entailed. The Special Ops Wireless Operators, who spoke German and many of whom had Jewish surnames or were from Eastern European descent, worked in isolation in a corner of the aircraft. Hidden behind a curtain and not connected to the crew's intercom system, they were under strict orders to abstain from discussing their work with anyone. Even their crew mates were left guessing, piecing things together about the exact role of the ABC.

The work was perilous beyond measure. 101 Squadron swiftly gained a reputation as one of the most heavily targeted units in Bomber Command. The odds of survival were stark; fewer than one in four aircrew members made it through unscathed. Those who endured six weeks of operations were granted a well-earned two-week leave, offering a brief respite from the relentless danger. Completing thirty missions, an extraordinary feat, earned them six months of leave and the option to transfer to the comparatively safer duties of ground crew.

The losses incurred by 101 Squadron were among the

highest in Bomber Command, with 1,176 airmen lost in action. And yet, the young men of this unit carried on with extraordinary courage, knowing their work was vital to the war effort. For Albert, those nights in the freezing skies above Europe must have been a heady mix of adrenaline, fear, and an overwhelming sense of purpose.

The legacy of 101 Squadron's special operations is one of bravery, innovation and sacrifice. Albert and his comrades were part of a pioneering effort that directly contributed to the eventual defeat of Nazi Germany. For a young man of twenty-two, it must have been an unforgettable, life-defining chapter; one of danger, duty, and a profound sense of being part of something far greater than himself.

6.1   Bomber Boys at Base

Life on the base at RAF Ludford Magna was spartan. The Nissen huts were cold and basic. They were corrugated iron shells, curved like half-buried pipes, with just two windows at one end to let in light. In winter, the damp crept in, and in summer, the metal trapped the heat. The only comforts were the stove in the middle, their warm beds, and the camaraderie of the men.

The Sergeants' Mess was the heart of the servicemen's social life. The bar was always lively with men letting off steam and laughter spilling out into the night air. Albert threw himself into it all: the horse play, the drinking competitions, and the ad hoc games. He even organised a football team when they had the chance to play.

For the first time in his life, he was surrounded by people from all over the world. Canadians, South Africans, Australians, New Zealanders all came together as aircrew, bound by a shared purpose. At first, their accents sounded alien to him, almost like they came from another world. But as they talked, laughed, and drank together, he realised they were just the same as him; young men caught up in the same war, facing the same dangers.

Then came a voice he couldn't believe, a familiar Northeastern accent straight from home. Flight Officer Weston Craig was from South Shields, just a few miles from Albert's home in West Boldon. It was the very place Albert's parents had met and married. The world suddenly felt a little smaller. Weston and Albert had much in common; they were just a year apart in age and would often reminisce about the places back home that they both knew so well. Their bond was a small piece of certainty in an uncertain world.

Albert's crew became his family; a tight-knit group forged by war, bound by trust, and strengthened by shared hardship. Though they came from different corners of the world, they relied on one another completely, each man playing a crucial role in keeping their Lancaster and each other safe.

Flight Officer Alan Lonsdale Lazenby – Pilot

A solid Northern man and a brilliant pilot, Alan Lazenby was the backbone of the crew. Born in 1915 in Guisborough, North Yorkshire, he was the oldest member of the team and brought experience and steadiness to every mission. Educated at Prior Pursgrove College, he had a sharp mind and a strong sense of duty. He had studied Art and been awarded a diploma. He married his sweetheart, Mabel, in 1939 in Scarborough, just as the world was on the brink of war. His leadership in the cockpit gave the crew confidence. No matter how dangerous the mission, they knew they were in good hands. Alan fully appreciated the dangers of war; he was under no illusions. His own father, Private Walter Lonsdale Lazenby, had been killed in action during WW1 at Flanders in September 1916, when Alan was just a year old. Alan's father was enlisted in the King's Own Yorkshire Light Infantry and buried at the Thiepval Memorial War Grave Cemetery.

Flight Officer Weston Craig – Navigator

Weston Craig was a fellow Northeasterner from South Shields, a fact that made his presence in the crew a special comfort to Albert. In a Lancaster full of men from across Britain and the Commonwealth, there was something reassuring about hearing a familiar accent, sharing jokes about home, and knowing that, even in the chaos of war, someone else understood where you came from.

Born on 16th May, 1922, Weston was the son of Robert and Jessie Craig. Before the war, he worked as an administrator in the Civil Service; a steady, reliable profession that reflected his naturally methodical mind. He was mild-mannered, kind, and highly intelligent, qualities that made him well suited to his eventual role as a navigator. His job was one of immense responsibility: guiding the crew through the vast, dark skies, across enemy territory and home again. Every mission depended on his precision and his ability to read the stars, the maps and the ever-changing weather conditions. A single miscalculation could mean missing the target, or worse, failing to find their way back to safety.

Interestingly, Weston had initially started to train as a pilot, but he later transitioned to navigation; a role that proved essential to his crew's survival. Cool-headed under pressure, he took on the weight of responsibility without complaint, earning the trust of those who depended on him in the most perilous of circumstances.

Sergeant Charles Lindsay – Flight Engineer

A Scott through and through, Charles Lindsay worked on the railways as a Clerk in Lanarkshire before the war. Affectionately known as 'Jock' to his crew mates, his careful attention to detail and friendly willingness to help his fellow crew mates made him a very likeable and popular member of the team. When it came to his job, though, he was all business. As the flight engineer, he was the one who kept the aircraft running, monitored fuel, troubleshot technical issues, and ensured their Lancaster made it home. Born in September 1922, he was the oldest of four siblings, two brothers and a sister all born and raised in Carstairs, Lanarkshire, a major freight railway junction for Scotland. His father also worked on the railway. This was a family not afraid of hard work.

Flight Officer James McClure – Bomb Aimer (RCAF)

James (Jim) McClure, one of two Canadians in the crew, was born in Winnipeg in May 1916. The oldest of four brothers, he was the pride of his parents, James and Mary, his father being of Scottish descent. Before joining the RCAF, McClure lived in St Vital and graduated from Glenlawn College. He was an avid sportsman who did well at whatever he turned his hand to. In the Bomber Crew, he was the Bomb Aimer, the man who guided the bombs to their target. His quiet confidence and steady hands were invaluable as he crouched over the bombsight, waiting for the perfect moment to release their payload. The weight of the mission often rested on his shoulders, but he never let it show. Analytical by nature and well-educated, Flight Officer James McClure was a fine asset to his crew, as well as being very popular and good company!

Sergeant Gerald Alfred Beckett – Air Gunner (Mid Upper) (RCAF)

Born in Regina, Saskatchewan, in 1917, Gerald Alfred Beckett was another of the crew's Canadian comrades. He brought with him a quiet determination and an easy manner shaped by the vast open landscapes of his homeland. Like so many young men from the Prairies, he answered the call to war, leaving behind the sweeping fields and big skies of Saskatchewan for a different kind of frontier: the deadly airspace over Europe.

Gerald's roots were firmly planted in Canada's pioneering past. His father, Alfred Beckett, had initially come to the prairies on a land grant and carved out a life in Glenavon, Saskatchewan. His first home was a sod hut, one of the rough-hewn dwellings built from thick-cut blocks of earth and grass—a necessity in a land where trees were scarce. These homes were cramped and rugged, barely holding back the harsh Prairie winters, yet they stood as symbols of resilience and survival. Life in such conditions demanded strength, resourcefulness, and sheer grit—qualities that Gerald would carry with him into his wartime service.

Eventually, Alfred moved his family into the city, where he found success in the automobile business. His roots stretched back to Manchester, England, and his ancestors, a family of engineers, had played a key role in the early industrial development of Hamilton, Ontario. Gerald's mother, May, also came from a family with an extraordinary past. Her great-great-grandfather, Paul Baghott, had once been a wealthy textile magnate in the Cotswolds, England, where he lived in the grand country house of Lypiatt Park. But he was a Luddite, resistant to the changes brought by the Industrial Revolution, and his failure to adapt cost him everything. His son, Samuel, had little choice but to leave England behind, forging a new life across the Atlantic.

In Canada, the Becketts and the Baghott families remained closely connected, so much so that four Beckett siblings married four Baghott siblings. It was a bond that ran deep, shaping the generations that followed. For Gerald, this meant growing up with a strong sense of family, hard work, and perseverance.

At twenty-two, he had not yet set out on a career path when war broke out, but perhaps it was no surprise that he chose to serve. The war was another kind of frontier, a new challenge that called upon men of courage and resolve. As an air gunner, stationed in the mid upper turret of a Lancaster bomber, Gerald's role was vital. He was the ever-watchful guardian of the crew, scanning the skies for enemy fighters, his finger poised over the triggers, always ready to defend his comrades.

From a sod hut on the Prairies to the cold, hostile skies over Europe, Gerald Alfred Beckett's journey was one of courage, sacrifice and the unbreakable spirit of the pioneer stock from which he came.

Sergeant Charles Derek Brown – Wireless Operator/Air Gunner/Special Operator

Derek Brown was the heart of the crew, always smiling, always lifting their spirits. A bright lad from Leamington Spa, he won a scholarship to Leamington College, where he studied German. That skill led him to be chosen for a secretive role as a Special Operator, using the ABC (Airborne Cigar) system to jam enemy communications. He responded to an appeal for German-speaking airmen, even though he had no idea what the mysterious role entailed. His work was vital but classified; even his own family wouldn't have known the full extent of what he did. Married to his sweetheart Doris in 1942, he "forgot" to mention to the RAF that he was married, and added an 'e' to his name (Browne) so he could volunteer for the Pathfinder missions, which were restricted to unmarried men.

Kindly shared by Derek Brown's niece, a great photo
showing Derek Brown 3rd from right in the front row,
supporting a rifle.

Sergeant Donald Henry (Donny) Stephens – Rear Gunner

At just nineteen years old, Donny was the youngest of the crew. He'd been brought up in a large, loving family of three brothers and two sisters in the Forest of Dean in Gloucestershire. His idyllic surroundings in rural England, interspersed with picnics and river fishing days, brought a lovely quality to life, in contrast to other members of the crew who were from the industrial heartland of the north. An excellent grammar school education at East Dean Grammar at Cindeford prepared him for the rigours of aircrew training. But behind his youthful features, he had already experienced deep personal loss. Donny's oldest brother, Trooper Albert William Francis (Alby) Stephens, had been killed in action in North Africa in 1941. Donny had another older brother, Steve, who was also serving in the RAF. Despite his age, Donny took his role in the rear turret with deadly seriousness. Night after night, he sat in the cold and iso-lation of the rear gunner's position, scanning the skies for enemy fighters. Affectionately known as 'Tail End Charlie,' the Rear Gunner had the essential role of defending the aircraft from attacks from behind.

Sergeant Albert A. Walton – Wireless Operator/Gunner

Born in May 1921 and from West Boldon, Co. Durham, Albert is the central character in this book. He was an excellent Wireless Operator and Air Gunner.

Together, these men formed a family in the skies, a mix of Northerners, Southerners, Scots, Canadians, and Midland-ers who trusted one another with their lives. In the quiet moments, they laughed, shared stories, and dreamed of the futures they hoped to return to. In battle, they were fearless, bound by duty and an unbreakable bond.

The process of 'crewing up' in Bomber Command was often an organic one. Unlike the rigid assignments of some military units, aircrew were given the opportunity to mingle and form bonds before officially becoming a team. In many cases, friendships were forged over a pint in the mess, a casual conversation in the barracks, or shared moments during training exercises.

For Albert and his crew, this process was no different. Some had arrived at 101 Squadron together, transferred on the same day from their previous training school. Each man brought a unique set of skills, but it was trust and camaraderie that made them a true unit. Pilots would naturally gravitate toward those they felt confident flying with, navigators sought out those they could rely on, and gunners looked for men they knew would have their backs in the heat of battle.

The Eight Crewmen

In researching this book, we've been incredibly fortunate to connect with the families of all eight crew members. Their generosity in sharing memories and photographs has allowed us to piece together the history of this remarkable crew. Seeing their faces side by side is a powerful and moving tribute. Sadly, one piece is still missing—we are still searching for the elusive photograph of F/O Alan L. Lazenby to complete this collage.

F/O Weston Craig

F/O James McClure

Sgt. Charles Derek Brown

Sgt. Donald Stephens

Sgt. Gerald A. Beckett

Sgt. Charles Lindsay

F/O Alan L. Lazenby DFC

Sgt. Albert A. Walton

Albert's crew came together not just by chance, but through a shared sense of duty and respect. In the early days, there were light-hearted moments with accents clashing, jokes flying, and realisation growing that, despite their different backgrounds, they were in this together.

The Canadians, Beckett and McClure, brought a quiet confidence, their voices carrying the warmth of home from thousands of miles away. Charles Lindsay, the likable Scot from Carstairs in Lanarkshire, had a natural ability to bring the group together, foster camaraderie, and lift spirits when it was needed most. Derek Brown's intelligence and humour made him a popular crew member and an invaluable asset. Weston Craig, from just a few miles from Albert's hometown, provided an unexpected but welcome reminder of home.

Donny, the youngest member of the crew, was someone the others instinctively looked out for. At just nineteen years old, he reminded them of younger brothers back home, and, as the only Southerner in the crew, he was on the receiving end of plenty of good-natured banter about the North-South divide.

At the heart of it all was their pilot, F/O Alan Lazenby. A steady and dependable leader, he guided the crew with a calm authority that inspired trust. Under his leadership, they became more than just a team; they became a tight-knit unit, each man relying on the others in the most challenging of circumstances.

As their training progressed, these individual friendships fused into something stronger. They no longer thought of themselves as separate roles – pilot, gunner, navigator – but as a single unit, relying on one another for survival. When they climbed into their Lancaster, they weren't just a crew. They were a family.

Market Rasen, Lincolnshire, the nearest town, felt different from Albert's home. In some ways, it was like West Boldon: small, close-knit, shaped by the land. But the people weren't miners or shipbuilders like the men Albert had grown up with. They worked the fields and spoke with a softer, rural accent. It took some getting used to.

Still, the two pubs in the village, The Black Horse and The White Hart, offered a change of scenery and a place to drink a pint of the regional ale, talk with locals and escape the reality of war for an evening. The airmen travelled around the village on bicycle, enjoying the freedom to explore the market town.

At first, life on the base had a strange excitement to it, almost like being on holiday. But that feeling didn't last. The missions came thick and fast. The intensity of their work, the dangers they faced, and the losses all bound the crew together. They weren't just friends. They were brothers.

Walton's time with 101 Squadron was as intense as it was brief, marked by incredible bravery and the ever-present shadow of loss. Over just three months, he flew on nine perilous sorties deep into enemy territory. Each mission carried not only the risk of death but also the heavy burden of knowing that, for some, the journey home would never be completed.

Summary of Albert's flights (Squadron 101):

- 18/10/1943 W4995 Hanover – 101 Sqdn lost 2 of 15 aircraft

- 20/10/1943 W4995 Leipzig – no losses

- 03/11/1943 LM364 Dusseldorf – 2 of 26 lost

- 18/11/1943 LM364 Berlin – 1 of 20 lost

- 22/11/1943 LM364 Berlin – 1 of 24 lost

- 23/11/1943 LM364 Berlin – no losses

- 26/11/1943 DV296 Stuttgart – no losses for Stuttgart, but 3 of 15 that bombed Berlin that night lost

- 16/12/1943 DV283 Berlin – 4 of 19 lost (one of the squadron's highest loss rates)

- 02/01/44 DV269 aircraft crashed close to Berlin. Four crew members died, four were captured and held POW

CHAPTER 7

RAF Ludford Magna – Home of 101 Squadron

Nestled in the Lincolnshire countryside, RAF Ludford Magna became home to 101 Squadron during World War II. Built as part of the RAF's expansion to accommodate the growing Bomber Command offensive, the station housed 1,953 male and 305 female personnel. However, the accommodation sites were widely dispersed across various agricultural fields to the north of the village, making daily life at Ludford Magna a logistical challenge. The station's technical site was located on the northwestern edge of the base, ensuring smooth operations for its heavy bombers.

Ludford Magna's operational backbone was its three concrete runways, laid out in the standard triangular pattern common to RAF bomber stations. The main north-south runway stretched 2,000 yards (1,830 meters), while the two secondary runways each measured 1,400 yards (1,280 meters). These runways were essential for handling the weight and firepower of the squadron's Lancaster bombers, which were loaded with ordnance supplied by No. 233 Maintenance Unit at RAF Market Stainton.

Battling the Elements – FIDO and "Granite"

Lincolnshire's frequent fog presented a serious threat to air operations, especially for returning crews struggling to locate a safe place to land after long and perilous missions. To counter this, Ludford Magna was one of the few RAF stations equipped with the early experimental FIDO system (Fog Investigation and Dispersal Operation).

The system consisted of seven large fuel tanks feeding petrol into two pipes running along the sides of the main runway. Once ignited, the open flame burners produced intense heat, lifting and dispersing the fog to reveal a visually clear and illuminated landing strip. Petrol was pumped through the pipes at 100,000 gallons per hour and ignited. The burning fuel created a dramatic spectacle, one that pilots described as both a lifeline and a terrifying sight as they approached through a corridor of fire.

FIDO in operation – Photo courtesy of the Imperial War Museum

In addition to FIDO, the station also relied on a network of volunteer observers positioned at surrounding posts. These observers were trained to fire coded, coloured rocket flares codenamed "Granite" to help guide aircraft lost in thick fog toward Ludford Magna or other FIDO-equipped stations nearby. Such was the importance placed on 101 Squadron's activities that Ludford Magna was one of the first air bases in Lincolnshire to be upgraded with FIDO.

"Mudford Magna" – The Perils of Poor Drainage

While fog was a major issue, it wasn't the only environmental challenge faced by those stationed at Ludford Magna. The airfield's poorly drained terrain quickly earned it the nickname "Mudford Magna" among weary personnel. Heavy rain often turned the grass-covered dispersal areas into a quagmire, making it difficult for ground crews to manoeuvre vehicles and service aircraft. Despite repeated efforts to improve drainage, the problem persisted throughout the war, adding yet another hardship to the already demanding conditions of Bomber Command life.

Yet, for all its difficulties, RAF Ludford Magna was a crucial hub of operations, playing a significant role in the bomber offensive over Nazi-occupied Europe. It was from this airfield that 101 Squadron launched countless missions, utilising their top-secret ABC (Airborne Cigar) jamming system to disrupt enemy communications; a tactic that made them one of the most effective yet most targeted squadrons in Bomber Command.

For Albert Walton and his fellow airmen, Ludford Magna was not just a place of service, it was also the launchpad for their perilous missions; a station that tested their resolve and a home where bonds of camaraderie were forged under the pressures of war.

7.1   Battle Order and Operations Room

In the daily rhythm of RAF Bomber Command during World War II, the anticipation of an impending operation began each morning with the posting of the "Battle Order". This crucial list, displayed prominently in the mess hall after breakfast, detailed which crews were assigned to fly that night. Airmen would gather, scanning the roster to see if their names appeared to mark them for the night's mission.

Once the Battle Order was digested, the tannoy system would summon the designated crews to the operations room. Here, they assembled before a large, curtained map of Europe. With a sense of gravity, the curtain was drawn back, revealing the night's target and flight path. The Commanding Officer, alongside flight commanders and intelligence officers, would brief the crews on critical details: the target's significance, the planned route, the formation, key landmarks, potential hazards, and expected enemy defences. Navigators meticulously noted course changes, wind speeds, landmarks, and flak concentrations, while pilots and bomb aimers marked their maps accordingly. The atmosphere was a mix of focused attention and underlying tension as the reality of the mission set in.

The hours leading up to the operation were a test of nerves. Airmen assigned to fly found it challenging to relax or divert their thoughts from the impending mission. Some penned letters to loved ones while others attempted to rest, but a pervasive sense of solemnity and wanting to get the raid started and finished overshadowed the usual camaraderie. The weight of their training and the uncertainty of what lay ahead pressed heavily on their minds.

Meanwhile, the ground crews laboured intensively to ready the Lancaster bombers. These teams were responsible for "bombing up" the aircraft, ensuring the correct ordnance was loaded, and "fuelling up," calculating the precise fuel required for the mission's range. Such a precious commodity was the 100 percent Octane petrol that RAF supplies were coloured green to deter theft and resale on the black market. Maintenance crews conducted thorough inspections, addressing any mechanical issues, repairing battle damage, and ensuring all systems were operational. Their dedication was paramount; the safety and success of the aircrews depended on their meticulous work.

In addition, Albert and his fellow crew members donned their War Service Uniform (Battledress), which consisted of:

- Helmet, with oxygen and communication mask
- Goggles
- Flying suit
- Mae West (life jacket)

- Parachute harness
- Warm sheepskin flying jacket
- Flying (escape) boots. These boots were designed to be cut down to shoes to enable being passed off as a civilian. There was a small knife concealed within one boot for the purpose of cutting.

Ensuring his escape maps and survival kit were securely tucked deep within his pocket, Albert felt the reassuring presence of a small yet cherished token in his wallet: his lucky 1919 thrupenny from Lily. The coin's date held special significance for Albert, marking both the year of his parents' marriage and the birth of his late brother, Norman. This tiny piece of silver, steeped in personal and cultural meaning, accompanied him everywhere, serving as a tangible reminder of home and the loved ones awaiting his safe return.

7.2   Superstition and Survival – The Power of Lucky Charms

For airmen flying combat missions during World War II, the line between life and death often seemed terrifyingly thin. No amount of training or skill could fully protect them from the unpredictable dangers they faced on every operation — enemy fighters appearing out of the darkness, flak shells bursting around them, mechanical failure, mid-air collisions, or simply being in the wrong place at the wrong time. Faced with such uncertainty, it was no surprise that many aircrew turned to superstition, creating rituals and holding onto lucky charms as a way of imposing some sense of control over their fate.

Superstition was deeply ingrained in the culture of Bomber Command. Many airmen developed their own pre-flight routines, convinced that repeating certain actions in exactly the same way could help ensure their safe return. Some would always climb into the aircraft in the same order, touch a specific part of the fuselage before take-off, or even wear the same item of clothing. Entire crews sometimes shared rituals, such as urinating on the tailwheel before departure (an oddly common practice among Lancaster squadrons), believed to bring good luck.

But perhaps the most enduring of all these superstitions was the reliance on lucky charms. Many airmen carried personal tokens, often small items gifted to them by loved ones before they went to war. Silver thrupenny bits, rabbits' feet, and miniature horse-shoes were among the most popular, but anything could take on special meaning if it had been associated with a previous successful flight. Some airmen tucked soft toys into their cockpit, while others swore by a coin, a religious medal, or a simple scrap of fabric.

Albert's Lucky Thrupenny Bit

Aircraft themselves were sometimes believed to carry luck, either good or bad. Some bombers gained a reputation for bringing their crews home safely time and again, while others were seen as ill-fated, avoided by those who had a choice. If an aircraft with a particular identification letter was lost too frequently, some squadrons would try to avoid assigning that letter to new aircraft. The number 13 was, as always, considered unlucky and some superstitious crews recorded their 13th mission as "12B" to avoid tempting fate.

Just as there were rituals to bring good luck, there were also strict taboos about inviting bad fortune. Taking a group photograph before completing a tour was widely believed to be asking for trouble. Airmen also avoided sleeping in the bed of crewmen who had been killed or wearing the uniform of a fallen comrade, fearing that to do so might seal their own fate.

Superstition even extended to personal relationships. Women who had lost more than one airman boyfriend were sometimes labelled "chop girls" and believed to bring misfortune to those they dated. A crew might pressure one of their numbers to end a relationship if they thought it was affecting their luck.

Interestingly, these beliefs were much stronger among bomber crews than fighter pilots. The reason was simple: fighter pilots, though they faced immense danger, still had the ability to take evasive action, using their skill to fight back. Bomber crews, on the other hand, had little choice but to fly straight and level through the storm of enemy defences, hoping that their aircraft would survive the barrage. For them, the war often felt like a lottery, and anything that might tilt the odds in their favour was clung to fiercely.

In reality, superstition made no tangible difference to survival. But psychologically, it was invaluable. It provided comfort and reassurance in an otherwise chaotic world, giving airmen something to hold onto as they climbed into their aircraft, night after night.

Whether these mascots really worked didn't matter; what did matter was that the crew believed in them. They gave each man something to cling to, something they believed would bring them back each time.

Approximately an hour before take-off, flight crews made their way to their designated aircraft, which were located in dispersal areas around the perimeter fence. This was a common tactic to reduce vulnerability from enemy attack. Clad in battledress, they carried essential equipment, including parachutes and survival kits. The aircraft were stocked with sandwiches wrapped in newspaper and thermos flasks filled with hot tea to sustain them through the long hours ahead. Each crew member assumed their station, conducted final equipment checks, and reported their readiness to the skipper. The pilot and flight engineer would then initiate the engine start-up sequence, bringing each of the Lancaster's four Rolls-Royce Merlin engines to life. The roar of the engines signalled the culmination of their preparations.

As the aircraft taxied to the runway, they joined a queue of bombers, each awaiting the signal to embark on their mission. The weight of responsibility, combined with the adrenaline of the impending flight, created a palpable tension. With clearance granted, the pilot advanced the throttles, and the Lancaster surged forward and lifted into the night sky, leaving behind the safety of the airfield and venturing into the unknown challenges ahead.

This cycle of preparation, anticipation, and completion of a sortie was the heartbeat of Bomber Command's relentless campaign and a testament to the courage and resilience of both the aircrews and the ground personnel who supported them.

The Life of an Airman: A Unique Wartime Existence

Serving as aircrew in Bomber Command offered a wartime experience unlike any other branch of the armed forces. While soldiers at the front or sailors often endured months away from home, airmen lived a life of sharp contrasts. One night they could be deep in enemy territory, flying through flak and night-fighter patrols to attack vital targets. The very next evening, they might find themselves enjoying a pint at a local pub in the peaceful English countryside of Market Rasen or attending a social gathering in the Sergeants' Mess at base.

It was a peculiar rhythm, with moments of intense danger and adrenaline followed by the comforts of home soil. Aircrew were well cared for: hot meals awaited them after operations, their quarters were warm, and every six weeks they received two weeks of leave. Deferred pay provided a financial cushion and allowed for some enjoyment during downtime.

Yet, the ever-present strain of their work lay beneath these comforts. Flying operations were not only physically demanding but mentally exhausting, requiring technical precision and nerves of steel. Despite the good food and relative comforts between missions, the looming uncertainty of survival hung over every sortie. It was this unique blend of danger, camaraderie and fleeting normalcy that defined the life of an RAF airman.

.

CHAPTER 8

The Sorties

18th October 1943 - Albert's First Sortie

Albert's first operational flight took place on the evening of 18th October, 1943, in Lancaster W4995. Flying with his regular crew, his target was Hanover, a heavily defended industrial German city and a key cog in the Nazi war machine. Its factories produced vital materials, oil, textiles, heavy armaments, and synthetic rubber, which made it a high value but treacherous objective. The Deurag oil refinery at Misburg was of particular importance as it supplied the Luftwaffe with thousands of tons of aviation fuel annually.

That morning, as aircrews gathered in the mess hall, the familiar ritual of checking the Battle Order took on a new weight for Albert. His name was listed alongside fourteen other crews from 101 Squadron, all scheduled to fly that night as part of a massive force of 360 Lancasters. He had known this moment would come, he had spent two years preparing for it, but seeing his crew's names in print made it suddenly real.

In addition to Pilot Alan Lonsdale Lazenby, the crew was as follows:

- Sgt. Gerald Alfred BECKETT (R/139887) Air Gunner RCAF
- Sgt. Charles Derek BROWN (1581033) Wireless Op (Specialist Operator ABC Radio)
- Sgt. Donald Henry STEPHENS (1586493) Air Gunner
- F/O. Sgt. Weston CRAIG (136365) Navigator
- Sgt. Charles LINDSAY (1566826) Flight Engineer
- F/O Sgt. James MCCLURE (J/22190) Air Bomber RCAF
- Sgt. Albert Avery WALTON (1496639) Wireless Operator/Reserve Gunner

The tension of the ensuing hours was almost unbearable. Every man had his own way of coping. Some wrote quick letters home. Others tried to rest but found it impossible to quiet their thoughts. Albert forced himself to focus on what he could control and ran through the mission details in his head — target, flight path, emergency procedures.

As the day wore on, ground crews worked tirelessly, preparing the aircraft for battle. The bombers were loaded with incendiaries and high explosives, and each crew was issued with survival packs and parachutes. The men ate their pre-flight meal of steak and eggs, a rare treat designed to fuel them for the long night ahead. It was a strangely silent affair; no one wanted to acknowledge the churning fear in their stomachs.

In the crew room they got changed into battledress. At times like this, a huge sign reminded them "eternal vigilance is the price of safety." The men couldn't help reading it often; there were a multitude of opportunities to practice it.

With all external and internal checks complete, they were ready for take-off. By 17:16, the sky was beginning to darken as Lancaster W4995 roared down the runway. If the aircraft was fully laden, the flaps were set at 25 degrees. The engines were gradually powered up as the pilot, Lazenby, pushed the throttles forward and held the aircraft against the brakes. At around zero boost, the brakes were released and the throttles pushed fully open, with the port engine slightly ahead to counteract any tendency to swing.

As the engines roared at full power, 3,000 rpm, they surged down the runway, the tail lifting as they gathered speed. The sheer force of take-off pressed Albert back into his seat, his hands gripping the edges of his equipment. In the confined space of the fuselage, the constant roar of the four Merlin engines was deafening yet strangely reassuring.

This was it. No turning back now.

Lindsay, the flight engineer, had to follow the pilot's hand on the throttles in case it slipped. At 95-105 mph, the Lancaster lifted effortlessly from the long Ludford runway. Once airborne, the order was given to retract the undercarriage. At around 800 feet, the flaps were raised, and they climbed steadily into the twilit sky.

It took three hours to reach the target. As they approached Hanover, the sky was thick with cloud cover, good for evading flak and night fighters, but a challenge for navigation. The Pathfinder aircraft, responsible for marking the target with flares, struggled to get accurate placements. The result was a scattered raid; only 50 of the 360 bombers hit within three miles of the aiming point, the rest dropping their payloads into open countryside.

Inside the Lancaster, Albert had little time to think beyond his immediate tasks. Eyes scanning his instruments and hands steady, he followed orders with precision. The rush of battle dulled his fear, replaced by an intense focus. They had trained for this, but nothing could truly prepare a man for the sensation of flying into enemy territory or the sight of flak bursts lighting up the sky or the knowledge that, at any moment, a night fighter could emerge from the darkness.

Somewhere in the chaos, other crews weren't so lucky. Of the fifteen Lancasters from 101 Squadron that had set out that night, only thirteen returned. Two were lost, shot down or forced to crash-land in enemy territory. No one knew their fate yet. Back at base, the emptiness of those missing aircraft would be a stark reminder of the risks they all faced.

Albert and his crew landed safely at 22:56, mission completed, aircraft intact, and bodies unharmed, but they weren't unchanged. The exhilaration of survival was tempered by the knowledge that others had not been so fortunate. After their debrief, they made their way to the mess hall where plates of bacon and eggs waited. Exhausted after the long period of intense concentration, they could finally wind down. It was a bomber crew tradition: hot food after a cold night in the sky.

The room was quieter than usual. Some men talked in low voices, replaying the mission in their heads. Others sat in silence, shell-shocked, grappling to come to terms with all they'd just witnessed, staring at nothing. Albert knew that he had crossed a threshold. He was no longer a trainee. He was an operational airman, a bomber crewman who had survived his first sortie. But he also knew that there would be many more to come.

That night, Bomber Command had reached a grim milestone: 5,000 aircraft lost on operations since the start of the war. Albert's first operation had been just one flight among thousands, but to him, it was everything. As he finally lay down to rest, exhaustion took over. He had made it through his first mission. But deep down, he knew that this was only the beginning.

Details From RAF Flight Log:

'Load: 1/4000 HC 3/1000 MC 48/30.840/4 (130c) IB Primary attacked at 2026 hrs from 20,000 ft. Heading 215T at RAS 150. 6/10 cloud over target. Visibility good. Bombed on centre of green T.I. Orange glow on cloud around markers. Incendiaries spread over a wide area. Large explosion seen in target area at 20.21 hrs. Raid too scattered to be a success.'

This sortie concluded the current series of raids on Hannover.

20th October 1943 – The Raid on Leipzig

That morning in the mess hall, just two days after his first sortie, Albert and his crew found their names on the Battle Order once again. Breakfast in the Sergeants' Mess was overshadowed by the long-distance mission that lay ahead. The ground crew were already hard at work preparing Lancaster W4995, ensuring it was ready for the night's operation. The target was Leipzig, and this was to be the first major assault on the city during the war.

Leipzig was a significant industrial hub for the German war effort. It housed multiple Messerschmitt aircraft factories producing Bf 109 fighters and a vital ball-bearing plant, and it served as a key transportation and railway hub. Disrupting these facilities would weaken the Luftwaffe and hinder the enemy's logistical operations.

With Leipzig further east than many previous targets, bomb loads were lighter to accommodate extra fuel for the long journey. A total of 358 Lancasters were dispatched that evening, with 350 reaching the target area.

At 17:15, just as dusk settled, Albert's Lancaster lifted off. Oxygen masks were donned at 10,000 ft as they crossed the East Frisian Islands and performed a 15-degree weave to evade anti-aircraft fire. After clearing the fighter belt, they resumed their climb, staying on track for the nearly four-hour flight to the target.

For Beckett and Stephens, manning the upper and rear gun turrets, it was an especially gruelling mission. Positioned in their cramped turrets, their roles required intense concentration for long periods of time. Every moment demanded vigilance, as their eyes scanned the darkness for the dreaded silhouette of a night fighter. Leipzig was defended by a formidable array of flak batteries and the lethal twin-engine Ju 88 and Bf 110 night fighters, all guided by Germany's sophisticated radar network.

The raid began between 20:56 and 21:34, with the bombers aiming for the city centre. However, appalling weather conditions made precision nearly impossible. The target indicators dropped by the Pathfinders were scattered by high winds, which led to a dispersed attack. Bombs fell mainly on the southern and eastern districts rather than the intended industrial zones and the mission was classed as a failure. On landing, the crew was whisked away to be debriefed via the locker room where the flying kit was deposited. The aircraft captain did most of the talking on these occasions, but the rest of the crew had their say if there was anything of note to report.

Snippet From F/O McClure's Flight Logbook

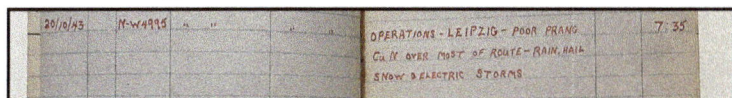

Details From RAF Flight Log:

'Load: 1/4000 HC, 48/30 840/4(+30x) IB. Primary attacked at 21.10 hrs from 20,000 Heading 1907T at RAS

158. 9/10 cloud over target, visibility poor. Bombed on ETA and small group of incendiaries. One Large explosion seen on approach at 21.00 hrs. Effort probably a failure.'

For 101 Squadron, the night ended in an extraordinary stroke of luck: every aircraft from the squadron returned safely. As Albert's Lancaster touched down at 00:50, relief must have swept through the crew. But they knew better than to expect such fortune to last.

Across Bomber Command that night, 16 aircraft losses were reported, 4.5% of the attacking force. Though the results of the raid were mixed, Leipzig would become a recurring target in the relentless strategic bombing campaign designed to wear down German industry and morale.

22nd October 1943 - Raid on Kassel

Albert awoke early that October morning to hurly-burly outside his hut. The noise! The hustle and bustle of ground crews preparing for the upcoming sortie had already disturbed the quiet, and, like many, he was irritated by the abrupt interruption of sleep. In the cramped space of the barracks, voices grumbled and muttered in low tones. From under his pillow, the broad Scottish drawl of his comrade Lindsay could be heard:

"Bloody groundcrew – wish they'd keep it down! Don't they know we could be up all night? Might as well get up for breakfast now."

At the mess hall, the air was heavy with both the aroma

of cooked breakfast and the underlying tension of an impending mission. The Battle Order list, pinned to the wall, detailed fourteen crews scheduled for the night shift. Albert's own crew was on the list.

Before the briefing, Flight Officer Lazenby announced, "We'd better make sure that bird flies before we set off for the night shift." He was referring to the necessary air test for the newly assigned Lancaster. LM364 had been away for extensive repairs following heavy damage the previous month. As the men tucked into their hearty breakfasts and chatted about the day's briefings and pre-flight checks, a stern voice boomed over the tannoy:

"Sergeant Walton, report immediately to the Personnel Office."

A knot tightened in Albert's stomach. What could this be about? His crewmates exchanged knowing glances and light-hearted jibes, expecting him to face some reprimand. With a mix of trepidation and resignation, Albert knocked and stepped into the office. There, Squadron Leader Rosevear explained that a telegram had arrived with news of his father, Alex Walton. A boatswain in the Merchant Navy, Alex had been rescued after his ship was torpedoed but had sustained severe injuries. His leg was broken, with flesh and muscle torn. Despite his return home, his condition was critical. In recognition of this family emergency, forty-eight hours of compassionate leave had been granted for Albert to travel home.

In that moment, Albert's focus shifted completely. The grim realities of war were momentarily eclipsed by the urgent need to be with his family. A swift alteration in the crew's roster meant that a replacement was to take Albert's place and a substitute Wireless Operator was assigned for that night's mission. Albert was instead to make his way home to West Boldon.

When Albert finally arrived at home, the scene was as heartbreaking as he had feared. His father, once a robust seafarer and pillar of the family, now lay incapacitated, weak, and gaunt. The injuries were life-altering: a broken leg, severe soft tissue damage, and the lingering scars of days spent clinging to life on a life raft in a stormy sea. Yet, despite the devastating state of his father, there was a fragile relief in knowing that he was alive, even if it had been touch and go.

At home in Boldon, his mother, Caroline, was over-come with worry yet mustered a determined hope to see her husband recover. Although the Walton family was no stranger to hardship and despair, this was a blow that went beyond what they had anticipated. Alex was not just a worker or a sailor, he was a hero in their eyes. Caroline loved him deeply and his condition struck a deep chord. Despite the overwhelming sadness, the family pulled together, drawing on years of resilience built during darker days.

For Albert, the compassionate leave was a bittersweet reprieve from his duties and a moment to confront the raw, personal cost of war. He carried with him the heavy responsibility of leadership and the ever-present memory of the sacrifices made, even as he faced the emotional toll of returning home to a family in crisis. He was so thankful to have Lily by his side to help him through this and, as he departed, he felt immensely cherished and hopeful for brighter days to come. He knew that Lily would support his family in his absence; that was all he could offer… now he was back to his other family to hear how they had fared without him during their mission on the 22nd. McClure's Flight Logbook summed up the day of two test flights followed by the evening's raid on Kassel: 'Good Prang, Clear conditions over target, Duff At Base, Diverted to Lindholme.'

Snippet From F/O McClure's Flight Logbook

3rd November 1943 - Raid on Düsseldorf

On the evening of 3rd November, 1943, Albert and his crew climbed aboard Lancaster LM364, preparing for another perilous mission. At precisely 17:05, they once again surged down the runway at Ludford Magna and ascended into the darkening sky, joining the fleet of bombers bound for Düsseldorf. This operation was part of a large strategic offensive by RAF Bomber Command involving 589 aircraft—344

Lancasters, 233 Halifaxes, and 12 Mosquitos. The objective was to strike at the heart of Düsseldorf's industrial and transportation infrastructure and cripple German war production.

Navigating through thick layers of flak and the ever-present threat of night fighters, the bombers pressed on.

The Bombing Run

Approaching the target was always a breathtaking sight with an inferno of anti-aircraft fire, searchlights sweeping the sky, and the eerie glow of marker flares suspended in the darkness. Fires raged on the ground below, while flak erupted in relentless bursts, forming what seemed like an impenetrable wall of explosions. It was in these moments the crew relied on the steady command of the Skipper, his calmness a lifeline amid the chaos.

As the bomb doors gaped open, McClure, the bomb aimer, took control, guiding them toward the target. The cockpit was filled with his constant stream of adjustments:

"Steady, steady, left a bit."

His voice was barely audible over the deafening roar of engines and enemy fire. Then, at last, came the call, "Bombs gone!" There was little need to announce it; the aircraft instantly lurched upwards, relieved of its heavy load, nearly throwing them off balance.

But the danger was far from over. With the payload released, they now had to endure what was often the most nerve-wracking part of the mission, the photographic run. A flare was deployed alongside the bombs, illuminating the target below just long enough for a special camera to capture the impact zone. The exposure time was unpredictable, requiring the pilot to hold the aircraft steady for an agonising eleven seconds. Every instinct screamed to break away, to climb and turn for safety, but for those crucial moments, they had no choice but to stay on course.

It felt like an eternity. Then, at last, the job was done. The pilot banked sharply, and the aircraft tore away from the firestorm. They were desperate to put as much distance as possible between themselves and the hell they had just unleashed. The raid inflicted widespread destruction, particularly in the city's central and southern districts, with factories, railway yards, and residential areas set ablaze.

However, the mission came at a steep cost. Eighteen aircraft failed to return, a 3.1% loss rate, each loss representing multiple lives – fathers, sons, and brothers – now missing, captured, or killed.

For 101 Squadron, the cost was especially personal. Two of their 26 aircraft were lost, meaning 16 airmen who had shared the same mess halls, training grounds, and moments of camaraderie were now gone. The uncertainty of their fates weighed heavily on those who made it back. Had they been taken prisoner? Had they perished in the flames of their stricken aircraft? Or had they somehow evaded capture, trekking through enemy territory in a desperate bid for freedom?

Albert's crew was among the fortunate ones that night, touching down safely at Ludford Magna at 21:45. The adrenaline of survival was dulled by the grim reality of those who were missing. The mess hall was quieter than usual, the predictable banter replaced by weary silence. The cost of war was becoming increasingly apparent, each mission leaving a heavier burden on those who lived to see another.

Snippet From F/O McClure's Flight Logbook

Details from RAF Flight Log:

'Load as above, including 1/1000MC. Primary attacked at 19.55 hrs from 22,000 ft. Heading 035T at RAS 160. Moderately clear over target, with some haze. Bombed on T.I reds. Large explosion seen at 1955 hrs. A good attack. Quiet route.'

9th November 1943 - Fighter Affiliation

On 9th November, 1943, Flight Sergeant Corkhill and his crew undertook a one-hour and ten-minute fighter affiliation exercise in their Lancaster LM369. Albert was part of this training exercise, which was a welcome break from the dangers over Nazi Germany. These exercises were essential for bomber crews to develop effective defensive manoeuvres against enemy fighters. An RAF fighter, often a Spitfire, would simulate attacks on the bomber to test and enhance the crew's responsiveness and coordination.

The ABC radios had just been introduced to 101 Squadron; no doubt, the crew needed training and familiarisation on equipment.

During these sessions, an instructor initially accompanied the crew, providing guidance on executing evasive actions, such as the "corkscrew" manoeuvre — a rapid descent followed by a sharp climb designed to evade pursuing aircraft. After initial training, the crew practiced independently, emphasising the importance of precise and vigorous manoeuvres to mirror real combat situations.

Each crew member had specific responsibilities during these drills. Gunners operated cine cameras mounted on their guns to record simulated engagements, allowing for later analysis of aiming accuracy and technique. The navigator maintained situational awareness and tracked the aircraft's position throughout the evasive actions to ensure a prompt return to the planned course upon completion of the manoeuvre. While the primary focus was on gunners and pilots, all crew members were vigilant, scanned for additional threats, and maintained internal communication to enhance overall accuracy.

These rigorous training exercises were crucial in preparing bomber crews for the challenges of operational missions, ensuring they could effectively respond to enemy engagements, and increasing their chances of survival in hostile environments.

18th November 1943 - Raid on Berlin

Then came Berlin, the ultimate test of nerves and skill. On the evening of 18th November, 1943, Albert and his trusted crew joined the first of several sorties to the Nazi capital. They took off at 17:40, just as daylight faded into darkness. Berlin was a fortress, bristling with anti-aircraft guns and crawling with night fighters.

Air Chief Marshal Sir Arthur Harris convened a conference to deliberate on the resumption of the strategic bombing offensive against Berlin. Recognising favourable weather conditions and the strategic importance of disrupting the German capital, Harris authorised a meticulously planned operation for that night.

The operation was characterised by a dual-target strategy, dividing Bomber Command into two distinct forces. The primary contingent, comprising 440 Avro Lancasters, was assigned to penetrate deep into enemy territory and deliver a concentrated assault on Berlin. Simultaneously, a secondary force, consisting of 395 bombers, 248 Handley Page Halifaxes, 114 Short Stirlings, and 33 Lancasters, was directed to target Ludwigshafen on Rhein. This diversion aimed to disperse German air defences and mitigate potential losses for the main attack on Berlin.

The Berlin raid commenced at 20:56 and concluded at 21:12. Despite the city's complete cloud cover, which necessitated blind bombing, the operation proceeded with minimal interference from German fighters. The Lancasters released approximately 2,300 tons of ordnance, comprising both high-explosive and incendiary bombs. The raid resulted in the loss of nine Lancasters, representing 2.0% of the attacking force. Berlin's police chief reported 154 fatalities, 443 injuries, and approximately 7,500 individuals rendered homeless due to the bombing.

Concurrently, the diversionary raid on Ludwigshafen faced challenges. The area was shrouded in cloud cover, leading to scattered and less effective bombing. German night fighters engaged this force more effectively, resulting in the loss of 23 aircraft – 12 Halifaxes, nine Stirlings, and two Lancasters – constituting a 5.8% loss rate. Local reports from Mannheim, adjacent to Ludwigshafen, indicated that while some industrial facilities, including the Daimler-Benz automobile factory, sustained significant damage, many bombs fell outside urban areas, causing extensive damage to agricultural properties.

This operation marked the initiation of what would become known as the Battle of Berlin, a series of intensive air raids intended to cripple Germany's war infrastructure and morale. While the November 18/19 raid inflicted damage and showcased the Allies' strategic reach, it also underscored the formidable challenges inherent in executing large-scale bombing missions against well-defended and distant targets.

Details from RAF Flight Log

'17.40 - 01.25. Load 1/4000 HC 16/30 IB 450/4 IB. Primary attacked at 21.13. hrs. from 22,000ft. Heading 079M at IAS 160. Bombed on green TI. Very large explosion below green TI. Glow below cloud over area.'

22nd November 1943 - Raid on Berlin

Just four days later, Albert returned to Berlin. Near-perfect flying conditions were forecast: light winds and clear skies over England, with cloud cover over Berlin that would help obscure the RAF formations from German searchlights. Because of this, a more direct "straight in, straight out" flight path was used that evening. The low cloud over Germany also allowed for a concentrated bombing window of just twenty-two minutes. However, due to the weather conditions, crews were unable to fully assess the destruction they had caused. To gather intelligence, several Spitfires were dispatched the following morning to photograph the aftermath. The raid was deemed a major success; massive destruction had been inflicted on the city.

A total of 764 aircraft were sent out that night, primarily Lancaster and Halifax bombers, with Stirlings and Mosquitoes making up the remainder. Two Lancasters crashed on take-off, though thankfully without casualties. However, 26 aircraft failed to return. In total, 167 aircrew were killed, and 25 men were captured over Germany, becoming prisoners of war. Among the losses was an aircraft from 101 Squadron, another devastating blow to an already embattled unit.

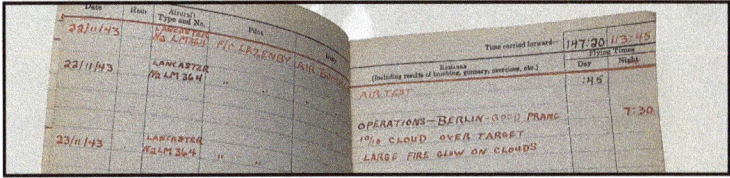

23rd November 1943 - Raid on Berlin

The very next night, the crews returned to Berlin for a second consecutive raid. Launching back-to-back operations presented an immense challenge for the ground crews who worked tirelessly to repair damaged aircraft, replenish fuel, and load bombs and incendiaries. Despite their efforts, over 100 Lancasters across Bomber Command could not be made ready in time for take-off. At Ludford Magna, the strain was evident. Ground crews struggled to fully arm all 19 Lancasters and several were forced to depart 2,000lb short of a full bomb load.

Albert and his comrades once again braved the perils of "The Big City," now battling not only enemy defences but also growing fatigue. A strong crosswind made take-off treacherous, yet, once in the sky, they pressed on.

Arriving over the target, the crew was struck by the sheer intensity of the anti-aircraft fire. Searchlights swept the sky in all directions, their beams crisscrossing through the darkness, while fires raged below, casting an eerie glow over the landscape. Coloured flares hung in the air, marking targets and adding to the chaotic scene. The flak was relentless, a wall of exploding shells that seemed impossible to pass through. In those moments, the steady composure and experience of the pilot was invaluable.

As the bomb doors opened, the bomb aimer took his position, scanning for the marker flares that would guide their run. By then, they were fully committed — deep in the heart of the inferno. The aircraft shuddered from near misses, the roar of engines and explosions merging into a deafening cacophony. It was like staring into the very depths of hell.

This time, against all odds, every aircraft from 101 Squadron made it home. Such nights were rare and must have felt like a fleeting blessing amid the relentless dangers.

Although 101 Squadron suffered no losses, several Lancasters returned early due to worsening conditions or crew exhaustion. Their pilots were met with sharp reprimands from the Wing Commander, who viewed their early return as "a bit shaky."

Across Bomber Command, 382 aircraft were dispatched that night. A further 26 aircraft were lost, with 127 crew killed and 24 taken prisoner.

Details from RAF Flight Log:

'17.07- 23.42 Load as above. Primary attacked 2007 hrs. from 22,000ft hdg 100M, IAS 165, 9/10 St.Ou. at approximately 12,000ft. Bombed red flares with green stars. Large explosions seen approx 20.15 hours.'

26th November 1943 - Raid on Stuttgart

On the night of November 26th, Albert and his usual crew piloted Lancaster DV296 on a mission targeting Stuttgart. This operation was part of a diversionary tactic designed to draw German night fighters away from the primary assault on Berlin. The raid on Stuttgart involved 178 bombers, predominantly Halifaxes, which conducted a scattered attack resulting in 31 civilian deaths and 156 injuries. The operation incurred the loss of six Halifaxes to enemy defences.

Simultaneously, the main force of 450 bombers was dispatched to Berlin. The Berlin raid faced significant challenges, including effective German air defences and adverse weather conditions, leading to the loss of 28 Lancasters, approximately 6.2% of the attacking force.

Upon their safe return from Stuttgart, Albert and his crew were met with the sombre news that three fellow aircraft assigned to the Berlin operation had been lost. The uncertainty surrounding the fate of their comrades, whether killed, captured, or forced to parachute into enemy territory, cast a palpable shadow over the squadron. The juxtaposition of their own safe return with the absence of their peers underscored the ever-present risks of their missions and deepened the bonds among the surviving crew members.

Snippet from F/O McClure's Flight Logbook

Details from RAF Flight Log:

17.29 - 00.59. Load 1 x 4000lb.HC. 930 x 4lb (90x) 56 x 30lb.HC. Primary attacked at 20.35 hours from 19,000ft, heading 186M at 165 RAS. Layer of thin S.C. tops 8/10, 10,000ft; large fires in built up areas.

10th December 1943 - Cross Country Flight

Of course, qualification was only the beginning. Aircrew underwent continuous Operational Training flights to ensure they were fully prepared for front-line duties. Specialist courses kept them up to date with the latest technical developments and changes in operational procedures, as aerial warfare evolved rapidly. The intensity of training was unrelenting, which reinforced teamwork, refined technical skills, and prepared crews for the physical and psychological demands of combat flying.

Building on the previous month's training exercises, Albert participated in a five-hour cross-country training flight on 10th December, 1943, aboard LM369 with Skipper F/S Corkhill. This flight likely served multiple purposes, including navigation practice, crew coordination, and familiarisation with the Airborne Cigar (ABC) radio jamming system. ABC was a cutting-edge electronic warfare tool designed to disrupt German night fighter communications, offering an essential advantage in the escalating bomber offensive. Mastery of this technology was vital for Albert's fellow Special Operator, as its effectiveness depended on precise operation under combat conditions.

In addition to ABC training, the flight also included bomb-aiming drills, which was an essential skill for successful raids. Instead of live ordnance, crews used practice bombs, often small concrete-filled casings or smoke markers, to hone their accuracy. These exercises were typically conducted over designated bombing ranges, where instructors assessed the results and provided feedback to improve performance. The practice was crucial, as a well-placed bomb load could determine the success of a mission, while a misplaced one could mean wasted effort or unnecessary civilian casualties.

Training flights like these also reinforced the crew's ability to operate as a cohesive unit. Each member had to perform their role with precision, from navigation and communication to defensive gunnery and bomb targeting. The long hours spent in training meant that when the time came for an operational sortie, every action would be second nature. With missions increasing in intensity and risk, this preparation could mean the difference between life and death.

CHAPTER 9

"Abandon Aircraft!"

The morning of 16th December, 1943, Lazenby and his crew hurried across the rain-soaked airfield toward the mess hall, holding old newspapers over their heads for shelter. The steady hum of activity around them was unmistakable. Ground crews were already hard at work, refuelling Lancasters and loading bombs off open trailers hauled in by tractors. It was a sure sign that a raid was planned for the evening. It was to be the first in nearly two weeks after winter weather had kept operations grounded.

The mess hall buzzed with movement, a steady stream of airmen coming and going. It had been three weeks since Albert had last flown an op, and the routine of camp life had started to wear thin. But as the smell of bacon and eggs mixed with the ever-present scent of aviation fuel, he felt a spring in his step and a familiar rush of anticipation.

As they entered, crews on their way out exchanged the usual morning banter. Albert grinned at the men as they strolled past, patting their stomachs.

"Hope you left some for us!" Albert called.

"Not a chance," they laughed. "We ate the lot!"

Inside, the crew gathered around the Battle Order list, scanning the names of those set to fly that night. Suddenly,

Lazenby's voice rang out.

"We're on for tonight, lads!"

A ripple of excitement ran through the group. Seventeen Lancasters were on the list. They didn't know where they were headed. But one thing was certain: it was going to be a cold, wet night in the skies over enemy territory. Due to worsening weather conditions, the sortie was brought forward.

The usual eight-man crew of DV283, skippered by Flight Officer Alan Lonsdale Lazenby, set off for Berlin at 16:17 from Ludford Magna, the air base for 101 Squadron, along with almost 500 other bombers. Such an early take-off time meant the sun was still up, which was a welcome but unusual occurrence.

Looking at the squadron's Operations Logbook, it's evident that this was a crew that flew together often. Not only did they know each other well, they were an experienced team that pulled together to complete their mission. The events that followed and the adversities they faced no doubt formed strong team bonds.

This Lancaster carried a G suffix after the serial number, an oblique stroke separating the digits from the suffix letter. This was standard on aircraft carrying secret radio equipment that warranted guarded access and required a 24-hour guard when not in the air. Across Bomber Command, a total of 483 Lancasters and 15 Mosquitoes would be dispatched that night.

Weather conditions were extremely poor that December evening, with strong winds, rain and low clouds making for difficult flying conditions. The Met Officer at Bourn stated that the planned raids would most likely be cancelled due to the poor weather, but the operation went ahead. Little did they know what was in store for them.

Shortly after take-off, there was a problem with one of the engines in DV283. Flames and a long trail of black smoke were seen and the engine, one of four, was likely switched off. Lancasters were more than capable of flying on just three working engines. Nevertheless, they pressed on. This sortie was going to be more challenging than expected, especially in the terrible weather. Thirty planes aborted the sortie to return home early before reaching the target.

Carrying the usual payload of a single 4000lb high-capacity bomb, known as a "cookie," along with over one thousand incendiary bombs, DV283 successfully arrived at the target at 20:04. Bomb Aimer McClure guided the plane with precision, opened the bomb doors at the exact moment, then:

"Bombs away . . . let's get out of here."

There was no mistaking when the bombs had gone. Lightened by the release of the heavy bombs, the Lancaster jolted upwards into the night sky. Navigator Craig was on the ball, shouting a new course through to the Skipper. The red glow of fires below the clouds confirmed a direct hit; the mission was successful with all bombs dropped on target in a concentrated area. However, McClure was unable to capture photographic images as proof of their strike due to the low cloud cover. Although the flak batteries were in action, the cloud prevented searchlights reaching the bombers and increased the chances of returning home.

During the homeward journey, weather conditions across the east of England worsened, so heavy reliance was placed on the Gee radio navigation aid. This involved using radio beacons positioned along the route, each transmitting a unique Morse Code call sign that Albert could identify to guide them home to Ludford Magna. As they neared their base, they prepared for one of the most hazardous phases of the journey, the return-to-home territory. Mid-air collisions were a real threat in the crowded skies. Fatigue was setting in, but they had to remain sharp. Survival depended on it.

Visibility was so poor due to dense freezing fog that it was causing chaos during landing and a serious situation ensued. Listening in on his wireless, Albert relayed what he could hear to the rest of the crew via intercom:

"There's been a prang at 101-Ludford . . . Airstrip closed . . . hold current position . . ."

Other Lancasters across Bomber Command were also colliding on their home runways whilst attempting to land, blocking the airstrips and preventing the returning bomber stream from touching down.

A backlog of planes soon built up above Lincolnshire; hundreds of Lancs were stacked in the sky, circling their airfields, and Skippers desperately awaited a slot to land. Low fuel was now becoming a major issue for many of the awaiting planes. Parachute harnesses were buckled up in readiness and the crew got into position. In case of a crash landing, this would improve their chances of survival.

Although the newly developed FIDO system, designed to clear fog and illuminate the runway, was activated at Ludford Magna, home to 101 Squadron, they could not accommodate the number of planes desperately awaiting touchdown. Every crew was jostling for an early position to land.

Almost out of fuel, Albert frantically spoke with the control tower on the ground to make sure they knew the urgency; time was of the utmost importance. Already compromised, with just three working engines, they were at a dangerously low altitude and unable to gain height.

Radio communication from base gave a glimmer of hope and ordered a number of aircraft to divert to nearby RAF stations. DV283 was instructed to reroute to RAF Faldingworth, which had three runways and was just a short distance from Ludford Magna. Albert quickly helped the navigator, F/O Craig, plot a new course and shouted the coordinates to the Skipper.

At that point, the engines began to splutter and, one by one, they stopped turning. Flight Engineer Sgt. Lindsay confirmed:

"We're out of juice."

The familiar loud rumble of the Merlin engines was now replaced with just the noise of the howling wind from outside; they were gliding towards the ground. Reality hit. Albert felt sick to the core. The crew readied themselves; they had trained for this situation, and they all knew what was coming.

At just 2,500 ft, it was now or never. Skipper Flight Officer Lazenby had no option but to give the order to abandon the aircraft, shouting:

"Parachute, parachute, prepare to bale out."

McClure hastily unlatched the escape hatch and threw it out of the stricken aircraft. With no time to waste, all eight crew were ready and scrambled out into the freezing night, into the pitch dark, engulfed by swirling dense clouds. One by one they pulled their ripcords, making a pistol-like crack as their chutes opened. The descent felt like it took ages; time stood still. The thick cloud cover obscured their view of each other and, for a few harrowing moments, each man was utterly alone, plummeting into darkness.

Then—bump!—a hard landing took Albert by surprise. He had not been able to gauge the approaching ground due to fog and darkness. Miraculously, all eight crewmen made it safely to the ground in one piece. The crewless aircraft was destroyed moments later when it crashed at Blackthorne Hill Farm at 00:14. The glow of the burning bomber wreckage lit up the night sky, a stark and final end to their mission.

Where the hell were they? The landscape around them was unfamiliar, dark and bitterly cold. Their bodies ached from the violent bale out and the adrenaline that had carried them through the mission was beginning to wear off, replaced by exhaustion and the creeping effects of shock.

Scattered across the area, the crew began calling out for each other. One by one, voices emerged from the darkness, each man relieved to hear the others respond. Somehow, against the odds, they had all survived. Lazenby, Beckett, Craig, Lindsay, Walton, McClure, Stephens, and Brown, reunited on firm ground and in one piece. Unbelievable! What an experience to have gone through! But now came the next challenge—how to get back to base?

Albert had managed to radio their position back to the control tower just moments before the order to abandon aircraft. With luck, a search party would be dispatched to retrieve them. Best to stay put and wait. An hour passed, then another; given the chaos at Ludford Magna, no surprise. The damp and cold of the foggy night seeped into their bones, their flying suits providing little protection against the elements. They shivered. Their much-anticipated post-mission bacon and eggs were long overdue, their stomachs growled with hunger, and they were exhausted and cold; the shock of the night's events was beginning to set in.

Finally, just before daybreak, the rumble of an approaching truck and searchlights signalled their rescue. The relief was immense, but the weight of the night's events still loomed over them. As they climbed aboard the truck, the rescue squad gave them the first hints of what had unfolded that night. It had been a disaster, chaos—one of the worst nights in 101 Squadron's history.

It wasn't until they returned to base the next morning that the full extent of the losses became clear. Sergeant Cooper and crew had been diverted to an RAF base in Yorkshire; very sadly, due to the horrendous weather conditions, they crashed on landing. Only the two gunners survived the ordeal due to the protection from their turrets; they were both badly injured. Many aircraft had not returned. Friends and comrades were missing, some never to be seen again. The gravity of the night's mission sank in. They had survived, but the cost had been devastating.

Snippet from F/O McClure's Flight Logbook

The Morning After: The Debrief on Black Thursday

The air in the briefing room was thick with cigarette smoke and silence. No one spoke as the men of Lazenby's crew took their seats, their shoulders hunched under the weight of exhaustion and something deeper—guilt. The previous night's events played over in their minds on a relentless loop. The abandoned aircraft. The crash. It still didn't feel entirely real.

Skipper Lazenby sat at the head of the table, staring at his hands. He felt hollow. As captain, he was responsible for his crew. He had brought them home alive, but at what cost? His Lancaster, their Lancaster, was gone. The aircraft that had carried them through their missions, that had been their home in the skies, was now a shattered, burnt wreck somewhere in the countryside.

He replayed the flight in his mind, searching for a moment—any moment—when he could have made a different choice. Should he have turned back the moment they lost an engine? But the briefing had been clear: only turn back in an emergency. One engine down wasn't an emergency. Not then. And then there was the fog. That damn fog that had eaten them up.

Squadron Leader Peterson stood at the front and cleared his throat. "Gentlemen, last night was a disaster for Bomber Command," he declared in a measured tone. "We lost more aircraft to the weather than to the enemy." A heavy silence fell over the room; every man's gaze was fixed on the floor.

"Today, we will review each crew's decisions to learn from these events. Lazenby, please begin."

Lazenby exhaled deeply before rising. In his broad Yorkshire accent, he recounted the night's harrowing sequence: the initial engine troubles, the long, arduous flight back through an unrelenting fog, and the crushing despair as the aircraft struggled to find a safe landing amid near-zero visibility. He paid tribute to his incredible crew; all had pushed themselves to the limit and worked admirably. When he reached the point of decision—ordering the crew to abandon the aircraft—he paused, his voice soft and laden with regret.

"I had no alternative," he said quietly. "We did what was necessary." Despite following standard protocol, his words betrayed the inner turmoil he felt over losing the Lancaster DV283, a highly valuable asset equipped with state-of-the-art radio communications gear and, more importantly, the trust of his men.

Around the table, his crew shifted uncomfortably. The flight engineer's eyes revealed lingering thoughts of whether he might have stretched the engines' performance a few extra minutes. The navigator wore an expression of quiet self-reproach, haunted by the missed opportunity to locate a safer airfield. The gunners, who had spent the mission ever watchful for enemy fighters, now wondered if the most deadly threat had come from the ground. Each man wrestled with his own private regret and responsibility.

At that moment, the atmosphere in the briefing room shifted. Instead of the harsh rebuke one might expect, the senior officer's tone softened. "In situations where survival depends on split-second decisions, the choices made can be the difference between life and death," he said. "Flight Lieutenant Lazenby's decision saved his entire crew last night. His leadership under extreme pressure is commendable."

A murmur of agreement spread through the room; the crew knew he was deserving. Lazenby felt a surge of relief mixed with enduring sorrow. Although his decision was validated, the loss of DV283—a vital asset and a symbol of their collective hopes—remained a bitter reminder of the night's chaos. Then, the senior officer added, "Effective immediately, you are promoted to Acting Flight Lieutenant."

The unexpected promotion struck Lazenby as both redemption and a heavy burden. As the debriefing concluded, the men filed out in subdued silence. Lazenby lingered for a moment, absorbing the weight of their collective loss and the responsibility that now rested squarely on his shoulders. The memory of the damaged Lancaster, a machine that had carried so many secrets and so much promise, would continue to cast a long shadow over his future missions.

Though the day's debriefing ended, the events of that night were indelibly etched into each man's soul. Even as preparations began for the next sortie, the shock and sorrow from the disaster remained as a constant, unyielding reminder of the unpredictability of war. For Lazenby and his crew, every subsequent mission would carry the echo of that fateful night, when every split-second decision meant life or death and the cost of survival was measured in both lost machines and bruised pride.

The promotion, unexpected yet thoroughly deserved, resonated as a moment of redemption. In the quiet aftermath, Lazenby stood silently, absorbing the recognition of his leadership. It was a bittersweet victory, a reminder that even in war's darkest hours, the burden of command can forge heroes from those who dare to make impossible choices.

When the debrief ended, no one spoke as they filed out. The war wouldn't pause for their grief. There would be another mission, another night in the sky. But for Lazenby, for all of them, the shame of leaving their Lancaster behind would stay with them.

A heavy price was paid that terrible night, which became known as Black Thursday. In total, 32 Lancasters were abandoned midair or crashed during landing due to bad weather conditions or running out of fuel (four Lancasters were lost from 101 Squadron), 127 men died, and 34 were injured on home soil.

The quick thinking of F/L Lazenby to abandon aircraft DV283 certainly saved the lives of his entire crew, and he was later awarded the Distinguished Flying Cross, which was for act or acts of valour, courage, or devotion to duty whilst flying in active operations against the enemy. In recognition of his skill on that difficult night, he was promoted to Flight Lieutenant.

Clipping from local newspaper

D.F.C. for Scarboro' Airman

In the latest list of R.A.F. awards appears the name of Acting-Fl.-Lt. Alan Lonsdale Lazenby, R.A.F.V.R., No. 101 Squadron, who was born in 1915 at Guisborough, and whose home is now at Scarborough. He receives the D.F.C.

Educated at the Grammar School, Guisborough, the Scarborough School of Art, and the City of Leeds College of Art, this officer enlisted for aircrew in 1940, and was commissioned in 1942.

The official citation says: "One night in December, 1943, this officer was the pilot of an aircraft detailed to attack Berlin. Soon after the take-off one of the aircraft's engines became defective, emitting dense quantities of black smoke and a long flame from the exhaust. In spite of this, Flt.-Lt. Lazenby continued his flight to the target, which, despite difficulty in gaining height, he successfully attacked. When crossing the North Sea on the return flight it was evident that to complete the sortie the petrol supply would have to be carefully governed. By skilfully using his engines, Flt.-Lt. Lazenby succeeded in reaching this country. He displayed great skill and determination throughout."

The citation reads:

"On a night in December 1943, this Officer (Alan L. Lazenby) was the pilot of an aircraft. Soon after the take-off, one of the aircraft's engines became defective, emitting dense quantities of black smoke and a long flame from the exhaust. In spite of this, Flight Lieutenant Lazenby continued his flight to the target which, despite difficulty in gaining height, he successfully attacked. When crossing the North Sea, on the return flight, it was evident that, to complete the sortie, the petrol supply would have to be carefully governed. By skilfully using his engines, Flight Lieutenant Lazenby succeeded in reaching this country. He displayed great skill and determination throughout."

Image of Distinguished Flying Cross (Solid Silver)

The incident was later referenced by our grandfather, Albert Walton, in a poignant handwritten letter dated 10th August 1945.

'Returning from a raid on Berlin on the 16th of December 1943 all the members of our aircraft (Lancaster) had to bale out over England'

This was not the only occasion when Walton deployed his parachute to save his life.

CHAPTER 10

The Final Flight: Lancaster DV269's Sortie to Berlin

It took a few weeks before Albert and his crewmates were allocated a replacement Lancaster. He had enjoyed a short spell of leave at home in Boldon over the Christmas holidays, a welcome and very special time for Lily and his family.

Back at 101, the relentless bombing campaign wore on; the strain on aircrew became increasingly evident. Exhaustion took its toll, with men prioritising sleep over the usual mess hall revelry. The once lively squadron bars grew quieter, the laughter and banter replaced by a subdued, introspective atmosphere.

By the end of 1943, morale had sunk to its lowest point. Christmas, which might have offered some respite, passed with little celebration. The usual high spirits of the season were dulled by the weight of recent losses and the knowledge that there was no break from the relentless cycle of operations.

During what should have been a holiday period, crews were sent to Berlin three times, suffering heavy casualties each time. The sense of purpose that came from a successful attack helped sustain them, but on nights when the results were uncertain, doubts crept in. The men rarely voiced them, but inwardly, they began to question whether the sacrifices they were making were truly turning the tide of the war.

Shortly before midnight on 2nd January, 1944, Lancaster DV269 roared down the runway at Ludford Magna, bound for Berlin. It was the first sortie of the new year for the usual crew, piloted by Lazenby, and was Albert's ninth mission. A total of 383 aircraft were dispatched that night from various squadrons, all Berlin bound—362 Lancasters, 12 Mosquitoes, and 9 Halifaxes.

Flying conditions were terrible; the snowy runway had to be cleared before the raid could commence, thick cloud cover made the journey treacherous, and 60 planes would go on to abort before reaching their target.

Outside, the air was freezing, bitterly cold even by January standards. Inside the aircraft, the young men sat in the dim red light of the cabin, their breath visible in the poorly heated fuselage. The weight of their task hung heavy, as did the sobering reality of survival statistics. Most crews in Bomber Command lasted just seven weeks and for Albert, now three months into his operational service, the odds were beginning to catch up with him.

The journey to Berlin would have been tense but familiar. For hours, they climbed and cruised through the night sky, weaving around flak zones and avoiding detection by prowling night fighters. The hum of the engines and the periodic crackle of Albert's wireless provided the soundtrack to their grim work. The target that night was Berlin, a city well-fortified by anti-aircraft guns and brimming with searchlights.

High above enemy territory, Derek Brown sat at his post, monitoring the mysterious and powerful ABC, Airborne Cigar, equipment. His task was both technical and tactical: to seek out and silence the voices of the enemy.

In front of him, a cathode ray tube glowed steadily in the darkened fuselage. A line of light pulsed across the screen; this was the timebase, driven by a panoramic receiver scanning the same radio bands used by the German night fighters. Any signal being transmitted across those bands would register as a fleeting 'blip' along the line.

Derek's eyes were trained to catch those blips the moment they appeared. He would instantly fine-tune the receiver to listen in. If he heard German, he knew exactly what to do. With swift precision, he brought one of three powerful transmitters to bear on the frequency. A switch was flicked, unleashing a loud, warbling signal designed to obliterate the enemy's voice and scatter their coordination.

Once one frequency was jammed, he turned to the next. Each aircraft like theirs carried three such jammers and, with two dozen aircraft fitted with ABC spread throughout the bomber stream, the night sky could be filled with up to 72 jamming signals at once, each one a direct assault on the Luftwaffe's ability to intercept, coordinate, or respond.

It was a silent war within a war, hidden in the airwaves, where Derek Brown played his part, not with guns, but with soundwaves and static.

As they approached their target, the crew were fully alert, every man at his station, knowing that the most dangerous moments were yet to come. At the bombing position, Flying Officer James McClure expertly sighted the target, "Steady, steady, 30 seconds to go... left... left a little... Bomb doors open... Bombs away!"

Releasing their payload with precision. The bombs dropped away into the darkness below to hit their target well, and McClure directed Lazenby to hold their current position for 11 seconds while he took the all-important photographs. Business accomplished, the Lancaster climbed and turned for home.

For a brief moment, there may have been a collective sigh of relief—they had completed their mission. But their trials were far from over.

Disaster Strikes Over Berlin

On the southern outskirts of Berlin, at around 3:30 AM, the unthinkable happened. DV269 was shot by enemy flak. The explosion shook the aircraft violently, tore through its structure, and caused significant damage. There was a strong smell of aviation fuel, then flames—flames everywhere—licking down the inside of the fuselage and smoke filled the cabin. Alarms blared as the crew scrambled to assess the situation. Despite the chaos, Bomb Aimer Jim McClure later reported that the plane was still flying relatively level. But the damage was severe, and fire raged; Flight Engineer Lindsay later reported that the pilot, Alan Lonsdale Lazenby, had said he was wounded in the leg. He then made the heart-wrenching decision to give the dreaded command:

"Abandon aircraft."

Despite knowing that he would possibly be unable to get out of the plane himself due to injury.

Without delay, the crew prepared to jump. The parachutes were their only hope, but as Albert readied himself in the chaos, he discovered to his horror that his parachute had accidentally opened inside the aircraft. The fabric had been scorched in the fire and when he finally leapt from the stricken bomber, he looked up to see two gaping holes in the canopy, one three feet wide, the other 18 inches. He must have wondered if the chute would hold. Flak hailed in all directions, lighting up the night sky.

The freezing air hit like a wall as Albert fell from the intense heat of the burning cabin into the night sky. The adrenaline coursing through his veins may have dulled the cold, but the sight of the damaged parachute would have been seared into his mind. Miraculously, the chute slowed his descent just enough. He crashed through the branches of a large tree, which absorbed much of the impact, leaving him battered but alive. Albert would later recall, in one of his rare moments of reflection, that the tree had likely saved his life.

A Tragic End for Four Crew Mates

Not all were so fortunate. Five men managed to escape the doomed aircraft, but Sergeant Charles Derek Brown(e), known as 'Derek', tragically died during his descent; it is reported that his chute did not open in time. His body was later recovered and initially buried in a local cemetery before being reinterred at the Berlin War Cemetery. An investigation by the Red Cross was unable to determine the exact circumstances of his death.

Pilot Alan Lonsdale Lazenby, Air Gunner Gerald Alfred Beckett, and Air Gunner Donald Stephens remained aboard the aircraft as it plummeted to the ground. All three perished in the crash, their lives lost alongside the aircraft they had bravely flown into battle. Their sacrifices are commemorated at the Berlin War Cemetery, their combined grave standing as a solemn reminder of the cost of war.

The precise circumstances of what caused Lancaster DV269 to crash on the early hours of 3rd January 1944 remain uncertain, with two differing accounts providing potential explanations. In his own hand, Albert Walton, who miraculously survived the incident, wrote simply that the aircraft was "hit by flak over Berlin." Flak was a constant and lethal presence for Bomber Command crews, blanketing the skies over enemy cities with bursts of shrapnel that tore through aircraft, engines, and crews alike.

However, another account, supported by historical records, offers a different perspective. According to the Nachtjagd Combat Archive, Lancaster DV269 was shot down by a German night fighter, a Bf 110G-4, piloted by Oberleutnant Albert Walter of 1./NJG6. It is believed the attack occurred at 02:58, during the bomber's return journey after successfully completing its bombing run over Berlin. The night skies were chaotic and perilous, with an estimated 100 night fighters intercepting the bomber stream that night. Walter's aircraft delivered the fatal blow, causing DV269 to crash near Michendorf, approximately 10 kilometres south of Potsdam and southwest of Berlin.

Adding a further twist to the story, Oblt. Albert Walter himself would meet his end just weeks later. On 24th February 1944, his Bf 110 was shot down by a Halifax bomber from 420 Squadron RCAF, marking the cyclical and relentless nature of war in the air.

That evening 26 Lancasters were lost in the raid. 168 men were killed and 31 were captured and became prisoners of war.

RAF Flight Log for 2nd January 1944 states "Aircraft missing, no communications since take-off."

While the exact cause of the crash may never be definitively known, both possibilities highlight the incredible dangers faced by Bomber Command crews. Whether brought down by the relentless flak over Berlin or by the deadly precision of a night fighter, the tragedy remains the same: the loss of four brave crewmates — Lazenby, Beckett, Stephens, and Brown. For Albert and the three others who parachuted to safety, this harrowing incident was a stark reminder of the razor-thin margins between life and death in the unforgiving skies of wartime Europe.

Dedication from McClure's flight book

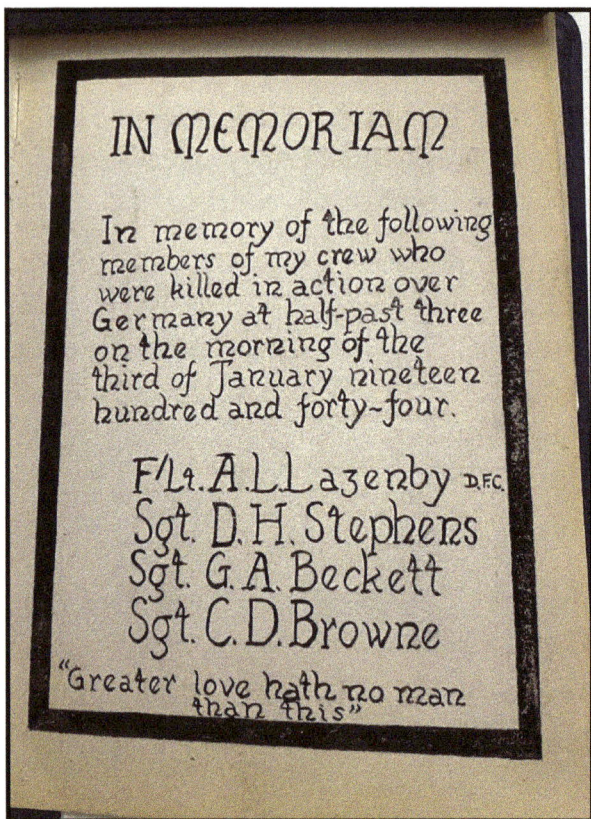

IN MEMORIAM

In memory of the following members of my crew who were killed in action over Germany at half-past three on the morning of the third of January nineteen hundred and forty-four.

F/Lt. A. LLazenby D.F.C.
Sgt. D. H. Stephens
Sgt. G. A. Beckett
Sgt. C. D. Browne

"Greater love hath no man than this"

Albert and the other three survivors did not know at the time that four of his crewmates had perished in the crash over Berlin. In fact, it would be many, many months until they knew the fate of the rest of their crew.

Flying together night after night, facing death as a unit, had forged an unbreakable bond between them. In a Lancaster bomber, you lived or died as a team. Each man depended on the others not just for success, but for survival. Lazenby had guided them through so many missions, bringing them home against the odds, his steady hands on the controls giving them confidence even in the most terrifying moments. Now he was gone. Beckett and Stephen, the two gunners, had remained at their posts, fighting to the very last as their crippled aircraft went down in flames. Brown had jumped but never made it, his parachute failing to open in time. Four men — brothers in all but blood — had been lost that night.

The uncertainty of their fate must have pressed down on Albert in the quiet moments and in the sleepless nights that would follow. How could it not? These weren't just names on a casualty list; they were men he had laughed with, fought alongside, and trusted with his life.

And yet, every airman understood the statistics. Survival was a gamble, the odds shifting with each mission. You could do everything right — fly the perfect route, drop your bombs with precision, defend yourself fiercely — and still never make it back. Death was not a possibility; it was a certainty, if not tonight, then soon. They all knew this. They had watched empty chairs appear at breakfast, bunks stripped bare in the barracks, and kit bags packed away, never to be claimed again. Albert had survived when so many had not. Did he question why? Did he feel guilty for making it out alive?

In the months to come, they found out the tragic result of their crash: four brilliant lives cut short.

Weston Craig, another survivor from their crew, had been deeply moved by the loss of their comrades. In the front of his logbook, he penned a dedication to the fallen — a simple yet powerful tribute to the friends he would never forget. It became one of his most treasured possessions; a testament to the bond they had shared. Albert, too, must have carried their memory with him, even if he never spoke of it.

Dedication from F/O Weston Craig's Flight Logbook

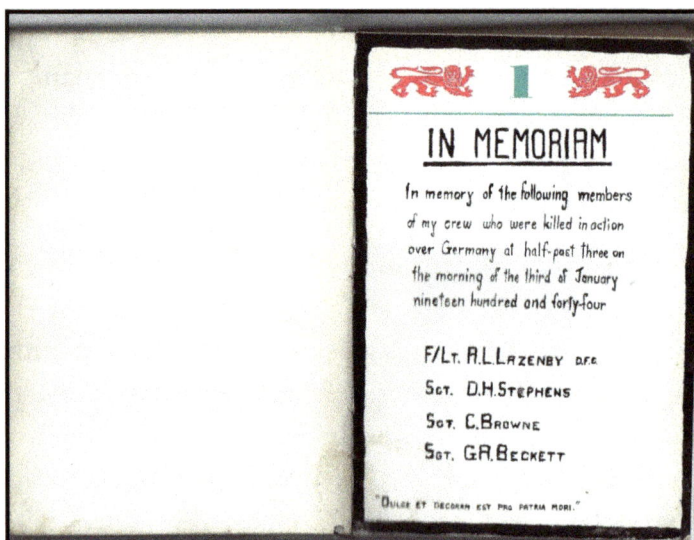

IN MEMORIAM

In memory of the following members of my crew who were killed in action over Germany at half-past three on the morning of the third of January nineteen hundred and forty-four.

F/Lt. A.L.Lazenby D.F.C.
Sgt. D.H.Stephens
Sgt. C.Browne
Sgt. G.R.Beckett

"Dulce et Decorum est pro patria mori."

Perhaps it was too painful to put into words. Or perhaps, like so many men of his generation, he simply chose to move forward. The grief remained, but life demanded to be lived. There were families to return to, futures to rebuild.

CHAPTER 11

Into the Shadows – A Night in the Woods

Albert slammed into the branches of a tree, his parachute catching in the tangle of limbs above. The silhouette of the burnt fabric hung conspicuously in the tree, a beacon for any pursuing Germans. Every moment spent beneath the dangling parachute increased the chance of discovery. Wasting no time, he wrestled with the harness and freed himself before dropping to the hard, frozen ground below. His breath billowed in the bitter air as he scanned the darkness. *Quick, find cover.*

He stumbled into the undergrowth, the world around him eerily alive with the distant sounds of chaos. Artillery rumbled like far-off thunder, the smell of fire was all around, flashes of flak lit the sky in sporadic bursts, and the faint hum of engines overhead marked the bomber stream already heading back to England. *Not for me*, Albert thought grimly. He was alone, cold, and in enemy territory. His stomach growled; there had been no time for supper aboard the Lancaster, but he quickly unwrapped a small portion of his emergency chocolate from his survival kit and let it melt on his tongue. It wasn't much, but it helped to calm his nerves.

Minutes stretched into hours. Where were the others? He strained his ears, hearing only the crackling of branches underfoot and the distant commotion of a search party forming. Spotlights swept across the sky beyond the treeline, German voices abruptly shouting commands. Heart pounding, he crept further into the woods, taking careful steps.

Far off, a dog barked. German soldiers called to one another, their voices growing louder. The thin crescent moon was veiled by clouds, casting the forest in near-total darkness. Good for hiding. Bad for navigating.

Albert fumbled with the tiny compass sewn into his trouser button, but the darkness rendered it useless. His silk escape maps folded in his pocket provided little guidance. Although he wasn't certain of his location, he was actually in an area called Luckenwalde, on the southern outskirts of Berlin. The only certainty was grim: he was deep in enemy territory, with no realistic route to neutral borders of Spain, Sweden, or Switzerland.

He moved carefully through the underbrush, branches clawing at his clothing. Time was slipping away. The cloak of night would soon lift. Exhaustion hit, hunger gnawed at his belly, and thirst burned his throat. Finding a patch of snow, he scooped up handfuls to moisten his parched mouth.

Albert's mind churned. Keep moving or lay low? Neither option promised safety. Albert wondered how the others had got on. He knew at least some had also baled out . . . he thought that at least five had jumped from the stricken aircraft but had no way of knowing the fate of other crew members.

As the first hints of dawn painted the horizon with cold, pale light, the forest seemed to hold its breath. Then, a snap of a twig. Voices, closer now. Dogs barking furiously. Albert flattened himself against the earth, heart hammering, the cold biting through his flight jacket.

A beam of light cut through the trees, sweeping closer. No more time.

A harsh voice rang out. "Hände hoch!" Hands up!

He had been found. Out of options, Albert slowly raised his arms. The dog snarled as two Landwacht soldiers emerged, rifles raised. Evasion was over. Albert's hopes of slipping through the night, of somehow making it back to Allied lines, faded with the darkness.

Captured, exhausted, and chilled to the bone, Albert knew that no matter what lay ahead, no matter how grim, he'd face it with courage.

Albert's Flight Logbook

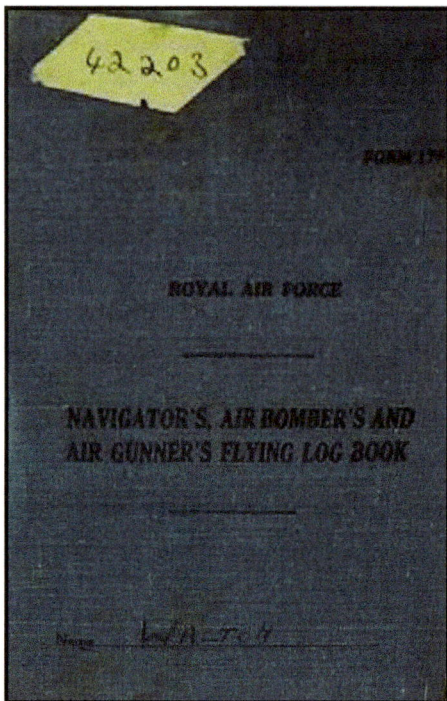

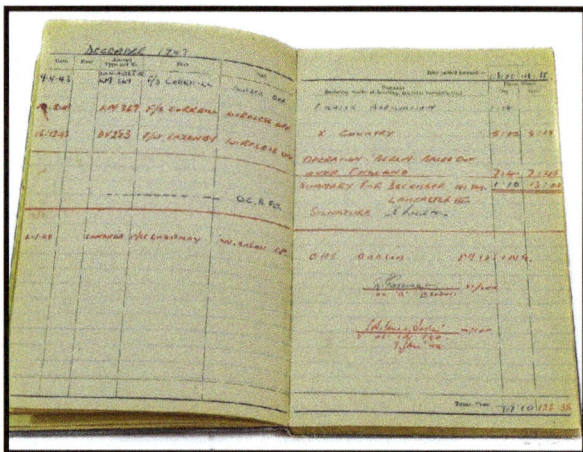

11.1 Capture and Survival

For Albert and three other survivors, Weston Craig, Charles Lindsay, and James McClure, the ordeal was far from over. Bruised and disoriented, they were all captured by German soldiers. The final moments of the mission must have played over and over in their minds as they were marched at gunpoint into captivity. For Albert, it marked the end of his active service with 101 Squadron, though his personal battle during the war was far from over.

These nine missions represent a story of extraordinary courage and heartbreaking loss. For every aircraft that returned safely, others did not. For every successful sortie, lives were changed forever, some ending in tragedy, others in capture, and a few in miraculous survival. Albert and his comrades carried this burden with them on every mission, knowing full well the risks they faced. Their sacrifices, and those of their comrades, were the price of freedom.

A Cohesive Crew

The men of DV269 came from different walks of life and corners of the world, but in the air, they functioned as a single unit. Whether it was Alan Lonsdale Lazenby's skilful piloting, Gerald Alfred Beckett's sharp eyes as Air Gunner, or Charles Derek Brown's expertise with the classified ABC radio equipment, each man relied on the others to perform their duties with precision.

The Lancaster's missions were demanding, but the camaraderie among the crew eased the weight of their responsibilities. They were bound by mutual respect, shared purpose and a commitment to one another—a bond that transcended ranks and nationalities.

Their final mission on 2nd January, 1944, brought this journey to a devastating end. Lancaster DV269 was brought down near Berlin. Four crew members were killed, while Albert Walton and three others parachuted to safety, only to be captured and held as prisoners of war. Though their time together ended in tragedy, the contributions and sacrifices of the crew of DV269 remain a lasting legacy of courage and teamwork.

Missing: The Aftermath of Lancaster DV269's Loss

Back at Ludford Magna, the rest of the formation began to return from the Berlin raid. Twelve aircraft had set out on the mission that night; one had returned early due to technical or mechanical difficulties—LM386, piloted by F/S Murphy, having first jettisoned their bomb load over the North Sea, was diverted directly to Exeter. Very often, crippled bombers returning from missions would divert into RAF Exeter for repairs and general maintenance. The sortie had been deemed a success; all eleven Lancasters from 101 had successfully dropped their bombs deep inside Berlin, striking the heart of the enemy. But for the crew of DV269, the night ended in disaster.

Radio communication with Albert's stricken Lancaster had been lost and their absence on return was both conspicuous and deeply troubling. At some point during the early hours of 3rd January, 1944, the grim realisation set in: DV269 would not be coming home. In Albert Walton's flight logbook, just three stark words would later sum up the mission: "Ops Berlin Missing." Those three words carried a world of meaning—grief, uncertainty, and the tragic loss of friends and comrades.

11.2   Captured by The Enemy

For Albert and his surviving crewmates, the nightmare of war was far from over. After parachuting into enemy territory, Albert was captured by German soldiers. Exhausted, shocked and shaken by the harrowing events of the night, he was transported to a building that he later described as being more like a village hall than a military installation. It was not a barracks or prison, more of a community space that had been repurposed to temporarily hold prisoners.

Inside the hall, there were other captured servicemen, all awaiting their fate. Among the confusion and tense atmosphere, the German soldiers began searching the prisoners. Albert was acutely aware of the danger he faced during this moment. In his pocket, he carried vital survival tools: silk escape maps issued to airmen, a tiny button compass and French francs—currency provided by the RAF to be used as bribes or for survival if ever on the run.

Quick-thinking and resourceful, Albert managed to take advantage of his position near a window in the room. Without drawing attention to himself, he discreetly slipped the items onto the windowsill, hiding them behind a curtain just in time. After being searched, he retrieved them; remarkably, they had gone unnoticed.

Albert's French francs, charred from the burning Lancaster

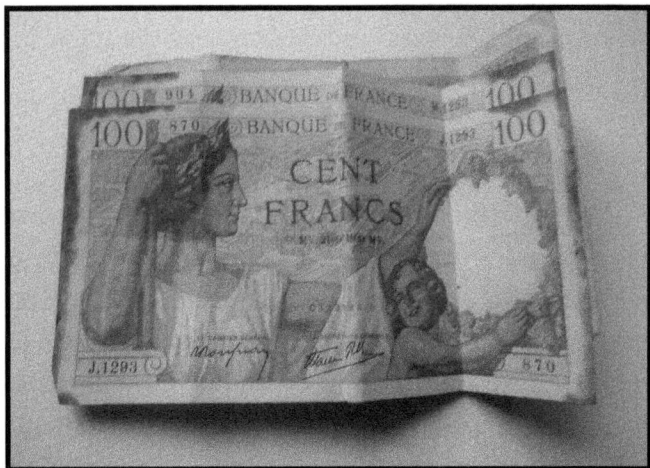

Later in the day, Charles Lindsay was brought into the same hall. Their eyes met. *Jock! Thank God*, Albert thought, realising that he wasn't alone. The sight of a familiar face and the knowledge that he was not the only survivor meant everything to Albert. We also know that McClure and Craig survived and were also captured. Before long, they were all being held at the same location, awaiting transfer, thus beginning their grim new chapter as prisoners of war.

The Relics of Survival

Today, Albert's quick thinking lives on through the arte-facts he preserved. The silk escape maps remain in perfect condition, still creased from when they were folded into his pocket. The tiny compass he carried continues to function, a testament to its craftsmanship and his ingenuity. The two French 100 franc notes tell a story of their own: their edges are scorched, bearing the marks of the fire that had engulfed Lancaster DV269. These relics are more than just objects; they are pieces of history, symbols of Albert's resilience, and resourcefulness in the face of extraordinary adversity.

Albert's original silk escape maps

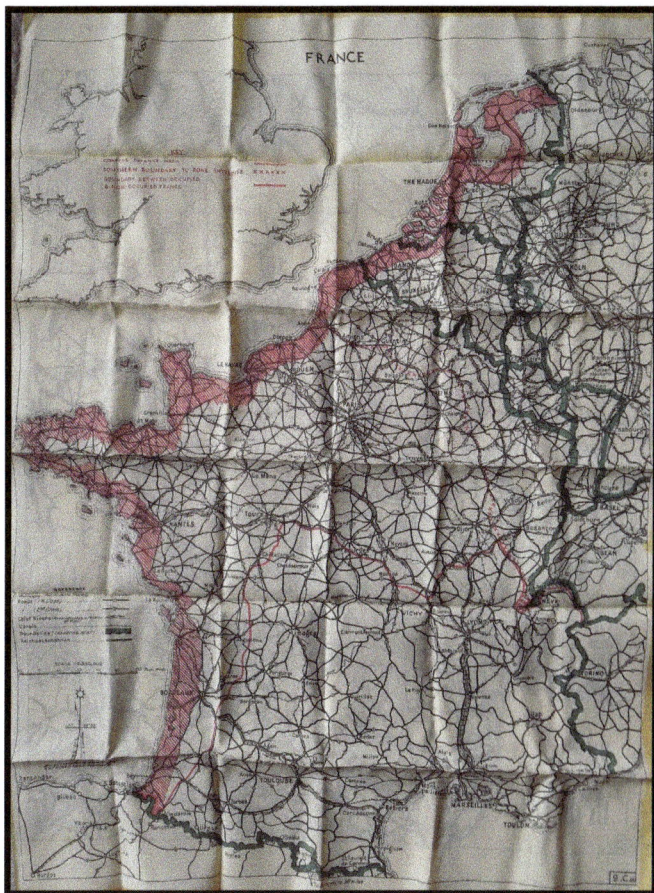

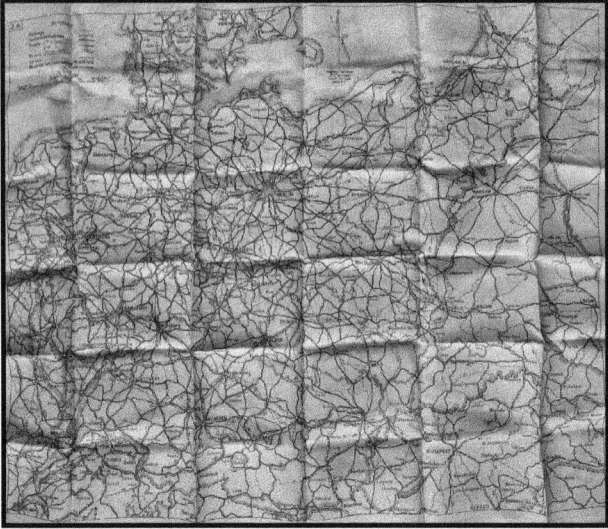

News Reaches Boldon

While Albert was navigating the terror of capture and survival, his family back in Boldon faced a different kind of torment. The dreaded telegram arrived, stark and unforgiving: Sergeant Albert Walton – Missing in Action.

No. It couldn't be. Not Albert. He was their pride and joy!

Caroline clutched the telegram, her hands trembling as she read the words over and over, willing them to change. Alex had only just survived his own ordeal at sea, his body still ravaged by injuries that would never fully heal. They were still grieving Norman, lost the year before. And now this? Another cruel twist of fate? Another son taken by this relentless war?

How much more was one family expected to endure?

Caroline fought to steady herself. She had to be strong for Alex, for the rest of the family, but the weight of it all threatened to crush her. Her daughters, Anne, Elwyn, and Hilda, gathered around, trying to console and support her, but how could they ease such anguish? They were barely holding themselves together. And John, her youngest son, stood silent, his face set with a determination beyond his years. Too young to enlist, he was now the only son left at home, and he felt the unspoken duty to be strong for his mother, to carry the weight of his absent brothers.

The house, once filled with warmth and laughter, now felt heavy with grief. Every knock at the door made their hearts pound, torn between hope and dread. Was it more bad news? Or, impossibly, a letter from Albert himself?

Days bled into weeks. The waiting was unbearable. Nights were the worst—long, sleepless hours filled with unanswered prayers and whispered pleas. The war had already stolen so much from them. Would it take Albert, too?

What they couldn't know, what they desperately needed to hear, was that Albert had survived. Against all odds, he had made it through. Though captured, he was alive. And one day, that truth would reach them, bringing both relief and an overwhelming sense of pride in the son they thought they had lost.

The families of the other missing crew members from DV269 would have received similar communications. Here is a copy of the letter sent to Charles Lindsay's father.

Lindsay's Missing in Action Letter

Royal Air Force Station,
Ludford Magna,
Market Rasen,
Lincs.

4th January, 1944.

101S/C.509/125/P1.

Dear Mr. Lindsay,

       I was indeed sorry to have to advise you that your Son, Sergeant Charles Lindsay (1566826) is missing from Air Operations, and it is with the sincere sympathy both of myself and the entire Squadron that I write you at this time.

       Your Son was the Flight Engineer in an aircraft which took off on an Operational Sortie over enemy territory on the night of the 2/3rd January, 1944, but I regret to say failed to return to base. No messages were received from the aircraft after take off and nothing has so far been heard of it or any member of the Crew.

       There is always the possibility that they may have come down by parachute or made a forced landing in enemy territory, in which case news of this would take a considerable time to come through, but you will be immediately advised of any further information that is received.

       Your Son had shown great keenness and efficiency in his work during the time he has been with the Squadron, and had become a popular member who will be greatly missed here. He was also a member of a very fine Crew and his duties have always been carried out with a splendid courage and determination.

       The personal effects of your Son are now in the custody of the "Committee of Adjustment Officer, R.A.F. Station, Ludford Magna", who will be writing to you shortly concerning their disposal.

       I feel most deeply for you at this anxious time, and we all join with you in hoping and praying that some good news will eventually come through.

Yours sincerely,

G. A. Carey - Foster,
Wing Commander, Commanding,
No. 101 Squadron, R.A.F.

Mr. G. Lindsay,
38, Coronation Street,
Carstairs Junction,
Lanarkshire.

CHAPTER 12

Life in Boldon During the War

The following are memories recorded by Jill Stephenson, whose grandmother, Doreen Walton, aged 97 at the time of writing, was the sister-in-law of Albert Walton.

During World War II, Boldon Colliery experienced its share of hardship and loss. The butcher's shop and the Co-Operative Hall were both destroyed by bombing, with the latter never being rebuilt. Many of the buildings that now make up the 'Flat Tops' once had a second storey, but after the war, they were left as they were—hence the nickname.

Albert Walton's mother, Caroline Mabel Walton, lived on Addison Road. She had an Anderson shelter, which she later dug up and repurposed as a garden shed. Nearby Davison Street and the street behind it were completely destroyed, while Fenwick's Row suffered severe damage but remained standing.

Despite the bombings, no one in Boldon was officially evacuated. Many locals believed that Boldon Pit, the coal-mining heart of the village, was a German target, but in reality, the Luftwaffe's primary objective was often the River Tyne and its shipyards.

Bombings and Losses

Incendiary bombs frequently fell on Boldon, lighting up the night sky. Doreen Walton recalled that Police Sergeant Matthew Slack in East Boldon was killed while trying to extinguish one.

The most tragic loss in the village was Iris Foster, who died the night before her 21st birthday. When the air raid sirens sounded, her mother and sister ran to take shelter under the stairs, but Iris remained at the fireplace, fixing her hair in the mirror. A bomb blast brought the chimney down, killing her instantly. Doreen remembered her as a very pretty girl. The family is believed to have lived next to the Co-op Hall on Hedworth Lane, which was also destroyed in the same attack.

A Plane Crash and the Brickie

During the war, a plane crashed near the Brickie—a pond on New Road, next to the Pit. The Brickie already had a dark reputation, as many people had drowned themselves there. Children were repeatedly warned: "Don't play near the Brickie."

Early in the war, Doreen, who was still a child herself, was looking after her little sister Nancy in a pushchair when the air raid sirens sounded. They had been visiting their grandmother, Annie Gault, who quickly sent them running home.

Life in The Pit and Air Raids

The Pit remained a busy, essential industry during the war. Every time the sirens sounded, coal miners were rushed to the surface as quickly as possible. Doreen's father, like many others, worked long shifts underground, but whenever a raid occurred, he would rush home in the blackout to check on his family.

One night, during a heavy raid, Doreen's father was at the Big Club on Station Road. He ran home in the darkness to Front Street (Colliery) to make sure his wife and children were safe. Along the way, he saw a blind man trying to find his way home to Church Street. He offered to help him, but the man smiled and replied,

"I could help you home; it's always dark for me."

That same night, the windows of the Smith family's home on Front Street were blown out. With no quick repairs available, the family lived upstairs for weeks, using make-shift wooden shutters covered with canvas which could be opened during the day for light.

Big Bertha and The Sound of War

Boldon had its own anti-aircraft gun, which locals called Big Bertha. It was stationed either on Hedworth Lane or somewhere near Jarrow. The children became experts at recognising the different aircraft sounds:

- The rapid rat-tat of British planes,
- The low drone of German bombers,
- The whistle and shriek of falling bombs.

Many families took shelter in Uncle Bob's stone-built bunker on Davison Street instead of using the larger, communal shelter at the top of the street. Bob had built bunk beds inside and, during raids, Doreen and her sister Nancy would huddle under blankets, trying to sleep, while their brothers, Billy and Bob, stood outside in the yard, watching the searchlights and tracers lighting up the sky. They would even commentate on the battle, cheering when Big Bertha fired at incoming German aircraft.

One evening, a particularly terrifying air raid began while little Nancy was in the bath. Panicked, she ran straight out, completely naked, into the shelter.

Final Thoughts

These recollections paint a vivid picture of wartime Boldon, a village struggling under the weight of war but standing strong together. From families huddling in shelters to fathers running home in the blackout, life in Boldon was defined by resilience, community, and hope.

12.1   A Prisoner of War

After parachuting to safety from the stricken Lancaster DV269 on 3rd January 1944, Albert Walton's war took a harrowing turn. Captured by German soldiers on enemy territory, he became a Prisoner of War (POW). Over the next 16 months, Albert endured the harsh and uncertain life of captivity in three camps, moving frequently before finding himself at the sprawling Stalag IV-B near Mühlberg on the Elbe River.

The Camps

Fourteen Days at Dulag Luft

The German soldier didn't speak as Albert climbed down from the truck. Just a gesture with the muzzle of his rifle: Move.

It was the 5th of January 1944. Albert had been a prisoner for only two days.

Captured after baling out of his crippled Lancaster over Germany, he'd been marched, guarded, and shunted across over 300 miles of rail and road, through bombed-out sidings and bitter cold, until he reached Dulag Luft: the Luftwaffe's main interrogation centre for captured aircrew, just outside Frankfurt.

All RAF aircrew had heard of it. Dulag Luft came up in intelligence lectures and whispered conversations. No one said much, but everyone knew it wasn't somewhere you wanted to end up.

Albert was just 22.

Upon arrival, prisoners were placed into solitary confinement cells, about nine feet long, six feet wide, and just over nine feet high. The walls were sound insulated; the small double windows were sealed. There was no view, no fresh air. The furnishings were stark: a hard wooden bed, a small table, a single chair, a bucket. Heat came from an electric radiator controlled by the guards, who could raise or lower the temperature at will.

Cigarettes, soap, and Red Cross parcels were all denied. The food was black bread, watery soup, and bitter ersatz coffee.

Geneva Convention rules allowed solitary confinement for up to thirty days. Most prisoners were kept for four or five. Albert would be in that cell for fourteen days.

The guards led Albert through gates and down corridors, stopping at a heavy steel door. It opened with a clang and closed behind him with the sound of a bolt sliding home. He was completely alone.

Solitary confinement doesn't break you all at once. It chips away at you, slowly, methodically. The first few hours passed in a haze of hyper-awareness. His instructors at RAF Faldingworth had trained him for this moment. It had been drilled into all of them to say nothing except name, rank, number. Nothing else. Repeat it like a prayer. Don't engage. Don't think.

But time worked differently in there. With no clock, no daylight, no voices, only the shuffling of guards and the echo of his own breathing. Albert began to lose track of the hours, then the days.

Sometimes the cell was stifling. Other times it froze. He adjusted physically. Mentally, he floated.

He sang softly to himself, snatches of RAF tunes, hymns from his choir days, old songs half-remembered from dances and pubs. He recited poetry from school and whispered the names of his crew like a lifeline, the whole lot. What about the four that weren't picked up… Maybe they all made it? Maybe they weren't gone. Hoping.

He thought of Lily, his love… worrying about her worrying. Thinking of his life in Boldon, how cherished he'd been… the colliery rooftops back home glazed with frost, the way his mother had said goodbye the day he left. The memories grounded him — just.

After what he guessed was the second or third day, they took him from his cell. Two guards led him to another room which was cleaner and better lit. A Luftwaffe officer sat behind a desk. He wore a polished uniform, spoke fluent English, and smiled as Albert entered.

"Sergeant Walton. Welcome to Dulag Luft."

Albert stood rigid.

"You're with 101 Squadron, yes? Out of Ludford Magna? You've been very busy over Berlin."

"Sergeant Albert Walton. 1496639. Royal Air Force."

The officer raised an eyebrow, amused. "Of course. Always so proper."

Then the questions began. About his aircraft. His crew. About the aerial fitted to the top of his Lancaster, the tell-tale sign of the secret Airborne Cigar (ABC) jamming system, used exclusively by 101 Squadron. About the German-speaking operators. The raids. The targets.

Albert gave nothing. Just name, rank, and number.

The Germans already knew far too much. The most unsettling part was how much they already knew without his help.

A day or two later, a guard handed Albert a Red Cross form to complete. It was, they said, "routine" for forwarding parcels and letters. It asked for his squadron, next-of-kin, recent operations.

Albert read it and put it down without filling it in. He had heard of these bogus forms, and he knew it was a trap.

The next time they returned, the tone had changed.

"You're being uncooperative, Sergeant. We cannot treat you as a normal prisoner if you continue to obstruct us. You are flying special missions, are you not? That is espionage. The Gestapo may wish to speak with you."

That word 'Gestapo' hung in the air.

Fear swept over him, cold and sharp. But he kept his silence.

Unlike some captured airmen, Albert wasn't physically tortured. But the threats, the isolation, the psychological pressure wore at him in its own, methodical way.

On or around the tenth of January, a guard handed him a pencil and a blank postcard.

A kindness. A slither of the outside world.

Albert wrote slowly, scraping words from exhaustion. Writing to his darling wife, trying to reassure her. He must have looked for some glimmers of comfort to pass on… directing Lily to contact The Red Cross for information on his situation and bizarrely saying "Jock and me are becoming good cooks, we cook all of our own meals." This comment is difficult to understand, as he probably hadn't seen Jock since the day of their arrival. Maybe he'd lost track of time. Or maybe he just wanted to give Lily something cheerful; a flash of domesticity, something to soften the truth, so she might imagine him safe, cooking potatoes with Jock and chatting about football. We'll never know. Maybe he did have periods outside of his cell to cook, though it does seem unrealistic.

He signed the postcard and passed it back.

Eventually, after 14 days the door opened. His time in solitary confinement, sometimes known as being 'in the cooler,' was over.

He was told he was being transferred to a permanent POW camp. They didn't say where.

As he marched out towards the waiting transport, Albert allowed himself a glance back at the grey concrete buildings of Dulag Luft. Just one look. No more.

Years later, he'd speak of it only briefly. "I'd been through the mill," he'd say. "But I kept my mouth shut."

What stayed with him wasn't one moment or one question, it was the silence. The absence. The fog that settled over everything.

And the knowledge that they had tried to break him — but hadn't.

Author's Note

This chapter is based on Albert Walton's own Liberation Questionnaire, official records, and the historical conditions reported at Dulag Luft Frankfurt. It portrays, with care and respect, what those fourteen days in solitary may have felt like for a 22-year-old lad from Boldon.

Our aim, as always, is to honour Albert and the crew who flew beside him, not just for what they did, but for what they endured.

Written on 10/1/44

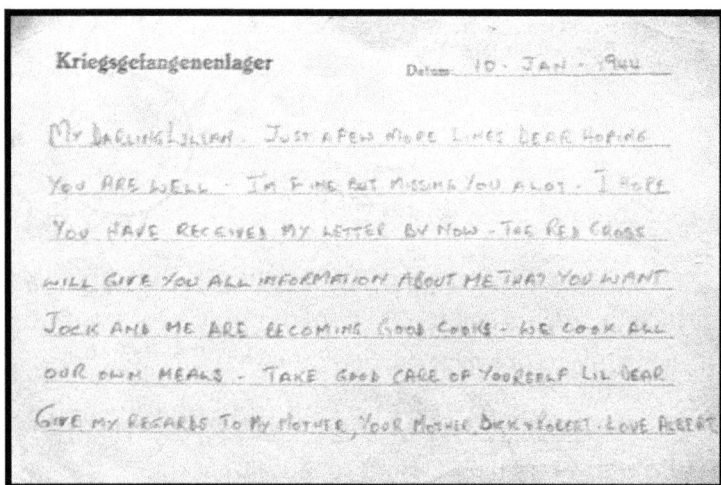

And another written 19/1/44

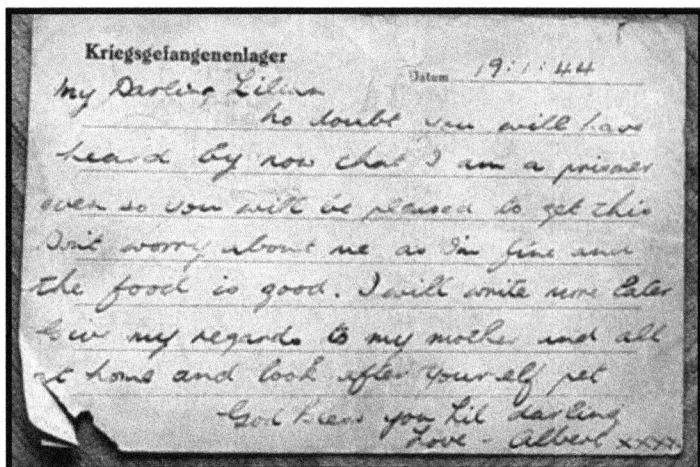

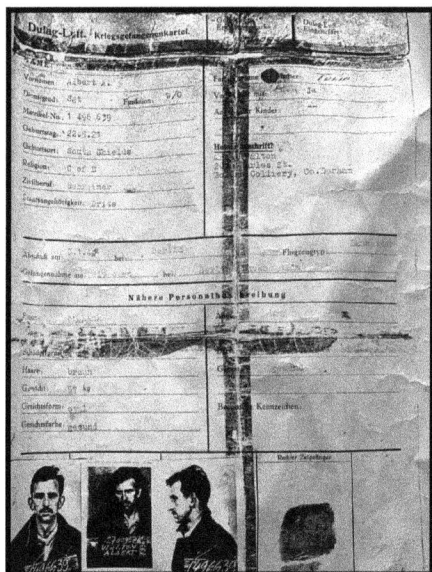

POW Identity Papers

From 19th to 29th January, Albert was moved to Dulag Luft Transit Camp, a holding station where POWs were processed and redistributed.

Finally, on 1st February 1944, Albert was transferred to Stalag IV-B, one of the largest POW camps in Germany. Located near the Elbe River, the camp housed tens of thousands of prisoners from across the Allied nations. It was here that Albert would spend the remainder of the war along with Charles Lindsay. Craig and McClure were held at a different camp, Stalag Luft III, which was specifically for officer airmen.

12.2   Word Reaches Home

News of Albert's fate reached his family in Boldon by late February 1944. A clipping in the Shields Daily Gazette, their local newspaper, confirmed that Albert was alive but being held as a POW in Germany. For his loved ones, it ended weeks of agonising uncertainty, though the knowledge of his captivity brought its own anguish.

A transcript from newspaper cutting: Shields Daily Gazette of 26th February, 1944.

Prisoner of War: Mr and Mrs Walton, of 10, Addison Road, West Boldon, have been officially notified that their son, Sergt. Albert Walton, R.A.F., is a prisoner of war in Germany. He has been posted missing during the raids in Germany in January. Walton writes to his parents that he is safe and well.

Aged 22, Sergt. Walton is a member of a family of eight. A married sister has been serving in the W.A.A.C. at Boldon for the past four years. Last year his eldest brother, Seaman Norman Walton, of the Royal Navy, was lost at sea when his ship was sunk by enemy action.

Sergt. Walton's father, who is an Estonian, has served in the Merchant Navy for 28 years and in the last war was torpedoed on three occasions. He has had similar experience in the present campaign and is now home on sick leave.

Sergt. Walton was married last year. He was formerly employed at the Bitumastic works at East Boldon.

PRISONERS

Mr and Mrs Craig, of 8 Louden Street, South Shields, have received the news that their son, Flying Officer Weston Craig, who has been missing for some time, is safe and a prisoner of war in the hands of the Germans.

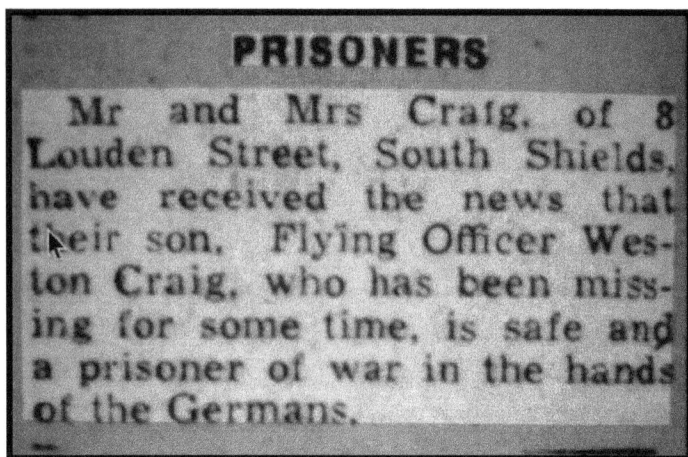

And similarly, Mr & Mrs Craig were notified in the Shields Gazette dated 9th of March 1944, that their son Weston was safe and a prisoner of war at the hands of the Germans.

"Mr and Mrs Craig, of 8 Louden Street, South Shields, have received the news that their son, Flying Officer Weston Craig, who has been missing for some time, is safe and a prisoner of war in the hands of the Germans."

CHAPTER 13

Life in Stalag IV-B

Stalag IV-B was the largest prisoner of war camp on German soil during World War II, established in September 1939. Over the course of the war, captured Servicemen from 33 nations passed through its gates, with the camp primarily housing Allied airmen, including British, American and French servicemen. Life in Stalag IV-B was marked by harsh conditions, overcrowding, and constant uncertainty.

Each day began and ended with roll call, when prisoners were counted in parades and huts were inspected by the feared "ferrets"—German guards tasked with searching for escape attempts or contraband. The camp itself was surrounded by double rows of barbed wire, with additional coils placed between the fences. A wooden rail marked the boundary that prisoners were forbidden to cross. The threat of punishment was ever-present, yet escape was considered a duty and much of camp life revolved around preparation.

POWs worked tirelessly to acquire maps, forged passes (Ausweis), civilian clothing, and tunnelling tools. Uniforms were dyed or stitched into disguises and forgery materials were improvised from whatever could be scavenged.

Despite the grim conditions, the prisoners adapted as best they could. The camp's Senior British Officer (SBO), a

Group Captain, enforced basic hygiene standards, encouraging prisoners to wash and shave regularly, even when only icy water was available. Occasionally, hot water was provided from the camp kitchens, though soap was scarce, often the crude German Ersatz variety or from intermittent Red Cross parcels.

To break the monotony, prisoners found ways to occupy their minds and bodies. Small vegetable plots sprang up between the huts, yielding modest crops of potatoes and tomatoes. Football and cricket matches provided fleeting distractions, though the playing field was often closed following escape attempts, such as the infamous Great Escape. Some huts were converted into makeshift theatres and libraries, with Red Cross boxes repurposed as seating. Theatrical groups staged plays, while a small camp band featuring a pianist, a trumpeter, a drummer, and several guitarists lifted spirits with impromptu performances.

Even in captivity, the British prisoners found ways to hold onto hope. Camp newspapers such as Flywheel and The New Times circulated news and morale-boosting stories, which were ingeniously handwritten on salvaged exercise book pages, using improvised inks made from quinine and millet soup. Meanwhile, letters from home provided a precious link to the outside world. From March to December 1944, Scottish prisoners even had their own periodical, The Scotsman.

Albert, trained as a carpenter before the war and may have contributed his skills to these projects. His resourcefulness, honed both at home and in the RAF, would have been invaluable in daily camp life.

Food was meagre, with German rations consisting of watery barley porridge and bread supplemented by Red Cross parcels, when they arrived. Guards frequently tampered with these parcels, puncturing tins to prevent hoarding. Ingenious prisoners melted solder from empty Fray Bentos tins to reseal the cans, ensuring their contents stayed fresh for longer.

Clothing was another challenge. Many prisoners had only the uniforms they were captured in and, over time, these deteriorated. Supplies from Red Cross parcels and captured British Army stores were rationed out, providing boots, wool underclothing, and American greatcoats. Albert, however, had one advantage: his sheepskin flight jacket, which offered some protection against the biting cold.

Lindsay's original "dog tags" from Stalag IV-B have survived to this day.

Holding On to Hope

Despite the hardships, Albert and his fellow POWs endured. Each day was a test of resilience, but they faced it with the same determination and resourcefulness that had carried them through their service.

Gardening Behind Barbed Wire – The Roots of a Passion

Was it in Stalag IV-B that Albert's love for gardening truly began? Perhaps. Amid the bleakness of captivity, gardening became more than just a pastime. It was a means of survival, a source of nourishment, and a rare slice of normality in a world confined by barbed wire.

Many prisoners found solace in cultivating small plots within the camp. The Royal Horticultural Society (RHS), in collaboration with the Red Cross, sent seeds and bulbs, allowing POWs to grow flowers and vegetables despite the harsh conditions. A horticultural society soon formed, with experienced gardeners among the prisoners giving lectures on cultivation.

Greenhouses and cold frames were built from salvaged materials and a makeshift boiler helped regulate temperatures. Against the odds, over 80 types of flowers, including sweet peas, chrysanthemums and dahlias, were grown, bringing a touch of beauty to the dreary camp landscape. Meanwhile, vegetables such as lettuce, radishes, pumpkins, cauliflowers, and potatoes provided vital supplements to their meagre rations.

The prisoners took their gardening seriously, even holding flower shows governed by RHS rules. Surplus produce was shared among fellow inmates or traded with guards for other necessities.

For Albert, this experience may have planted the seed of a lifelong passion. Whether it was the satisfaction of growing something from nothing, the quiet escape it provided, or simply the joy of nurturing life in the most unlikely of places, it was clear that gardening had taken root in his heart. It was a joy that would flourish long after the war was over.

The Beautiful Game - Football Behind Barbed Wire

In the sprawling, wire-ringed confines of Stalag IV-B, where frost crept in under the flimsy walls of the huts and spirits sometimes flagged with the grey monotony of captivity, something unexpected stirred the hearts of hundreds of Allied prisoners: football.

It might seem strange to imagine that, in a place defined by loss of freedom, the beautiful game flourished. Yet week after week, teams laced up worn boots, patched up their kits, and took to the rough, makeshift football pitches of the camp. These games weren't merely a distraction, they were a defiant act of normalcy, a momentary reclaiming of identity, and for some, even a source of pride.

Stalag IV-B, located near Mühlberg on the Elbe in eastern Germany, held tens of thousands of Allied troops during the war: British, Canadian, Australian, South African, and later, American and Russian prisoners. Among them were not just ordinary Servicemen, but professional sportsmen, including a surprising number of former professional footballers from English and Scottish clubs. In that unexpected melting pot, football emerged as one of the great levellers.

The matches were far from amateur knockabouts. Former professionals like Alan Steen, a Wolverhampton Wanderers winger, were among those interned at IV-B. While records are patchy, oral accounts and scraps of POW newspapers such as The Scotsman, produced within the camp, record matches played with remarkable organisation and competitive zeal. One such report describes an "England vs Wales" fixture in which England emerged 3–0 winners. Another records Newport County defeating Manchester City 4–1 – an impressive feat, even if only symbolic, given both teams were constructed from POWs who had once worn those club shirts in peacetime.

Many other matches were played at an amateur level, but no less enthusiastically! Games between different huts were commonplace: RAF vs Army and Amateurs vs Professionals can be seen in the records.

These matches weren't just for the players. Crowds formed from across the camp with spectators huddling together on the sidelines for warmth and a sense of fellowship. In those moments, for ninety brief minutes, the war seemed to fade. The guards looked on with amused tolerance, aware perhaps of the role football played in maintaining camp morale and making their own job easier by a population kept mentally and physically active.

Creativity was essential. Real kits and proper balls were rare luxuries. Prisoners made do, dyeing vests in team colours and crafting footballs from stitched-together scraps, rubber, and string. One RAF POW recalled dyeing a white shirt to resemble his club strip back home, taking pride in it as though he were stepping out once more into a packed stadium.

Albert Walton, a wireless operator before his capture, was a keen footballer and a capable goalkeeper. Though his name doesn't appear in the official team lists preserved from the camp, those records were far from complete. It's entirely possible and very probable that he stood between the posts during some informal matches, calling instructions to his defenders as he had once relayed coded signals in the darkness of the skies over Europe. Or perhaps he stood quietly at the sidelines, observing the game unfold with the same intensity he brought to his RAF duties.

What is certain is that Albert, like so many others, would have drawn strength from the spectacle. For the men of Stalag IV-B, football offered a connection to the lives they had left behind and to the lives they hoped to return to.

The matches carried on through 1944 into 1945, with leagues formed and teams named after their pre-war civilian counterparts. There was order in the chaos; fixtures scheduled, positions assigned, friendly rivalries sparked. The rules were enforced with rigour; tempers occasionally flared, but the game, always, brought the camp back together.

In the final months of the war, as liberation approached and the atmosphere inside the camp grew tense with rumour, the games slowed. Yet their impact endured. Long after the barbed wire came down, the men who had played and watched remembered those matches not only as sport, but as resistance, unity and the faint echo of home.

Footnote: Football Fixtures from the Scotsman POW Newspaper – Stalag IV-B

The following are examples of football fixtures and reports recorded in The Scotsman, a POW-produced newspaper at Stalag IV-B, offering a rare insight into the camp's vibrant sporting life:

England v Wales – A featured fixture reported with England winning 3–0, suggesting a structured national league-style competition.

Newport County v Manchester City – Newport won 4–1. Teams were composed of POWs identifying with or having played professionally for those clubs pre-war.

Celtic v Rangers – Matches between Scottish teams were a regular highlight, with detailed match reports written in the style of peacetime sports journalism.

Goal of the Month Column – Some issues included light-hearted awards for standout performances, showing the care taken to replicate normal football culture.

Player Profiles – Professional players like Alan Steen were sometimes profiled, often with anecdotes from their pre-war careers.

These fixtures were written up with flair and humour, often accompanied by cartoons and commentary and provided a mental escape for both players and readers. For POWs at Stalag IV-B, The Scotsman became more than a newsletter—it was a vital thread tying them to the world beyond the wire.

Curtain Up in Captivity – Entertaining Behind Barbed Wire.

In a prison camp built to extinguish spirit, music, laughter and theatre flickered like candlelight in the dark.

Stalag IV-B was a grim, overcrowded prisoner-of-war camp holding tens of thousands of Allied servicemen during World War Two. Men lived in cramped wooden huts, exposed to the brutal cold of East German winters, gnawing hunger, and the uncertainty of war's end. Morale was constantly under siege. And yet, somehow, amid barbed wire, illness, and loss, there were nights when the sounds of a jazz band echoed across the compound, or a crowd roared with laughter at a comedy sketch performed by men in borrowed wigs and makeshift paper costumes.

Entertainment inside the camp was no luxury. It was a coping mechanism, a fragile but fiercely guarded defence against despair.

One of the barrack blocks had been converted into a theatre by the prisoners themselves. The far end was transformed into a stage, complete with improvised scenery, makeshift lighting, and tiered bench seating for over 500 men. Though cobbled together from scrap wood, Red Cross crates, and blankets, it had the spirit of a real playhouse. The shows staged here, whether musical performances, light comedies or short plays, brought moments of relief and laughter to men starved of both.

Performances like Music in the Cage, produced by Leo Mundy and Frank Lazari with music arranged by Bill Irving, became legendary inside the wire. Les Whitmore's band, conducted by Alan Bolt, played whatever instruments they could find or fashion, such as violins strung with salvaged wire and drums made from tin cans. The camp orchestra played everything from swing tunes to classical pieces, drawing on the surprising musical talent hidden among the POWs.

Smaller "hut shows" brought this creativity into the living quarters. These were portable performances, variety acts, magic tricks, impersonations, and comic songs, all played on barrack floors, using curtains made from old blankets and props fashioned from food tins and broom handles. In the bitter winter of 1944–45, when fuel was scarce and food was short, these small shows offered a kind of medicine. Laughter wasn't just welcome, it was essential.

Albert Walton, a wireless operator before he was shot down, would never have called himself a performer. But he was a keen observer, and, like many of his comrades, he found deep comfort in these performances. Whether watching from the back row or standing in the cold outside the hut listening to the music, Albert knew the value of a moment when you could forget your stomach and remember who you were.

These cultural activities were the counterpart to sport, which also played a vital role in camp morale. Just as Albert had stood between the goalposts in RAF matches before his capture and later watched football tournaments inside the wire, so too did these concerts and shows give the men structure, dignity, and a reason to keep going. Both theatre and football offered escape, but more importantly, they reaffirmed identity and camaraderie.

The talent pool in the camp was rich. Among the prisoners were trained actors, musicians and even future writers. One, Claude Simon, would go on to win the Nobel Prize for Literature. Others returned to the theatre or music hall after the war. While not all names are known, their contribution to the mental and emotional survival of fellow prisoners was immense.

Camp newspapers like The Scotsman documented this cultural life. Satirical columns, cast lists, music reviews, and poetry appeared regularly in these hand-typed, mimeographed papers. One edition joked, "Tonight's curtain goes up at 19:30 sharp, unless the lights go out again." The wit was gallows humour, but the message was hopeful: we are still here, still thinking, still creating.

Even the guards, on occasion, attended shows or allowed extra time for rehearsals. A functioning theatre made for a calmer, more stable camp. But for the prisoners, these performances were never just a distraction. They were a declaration.

No one forgot where they were. But for a few precious minutes, in the glow of a hurricane lamp and the shuffle of borrowed shoes across a makeshift stage, the wire seemed a little less close.

Top Billing: Notable Performances in Stalag IV-B

Music in the Cage

A full-scale musical show produced by POWs Leo Mundy and Frank Lazari, featuring live band, comedy songs and chorus lines.

Hut Variety Nights

Travelling mini-performances including comic sketches, impersonations and musical acts, performed in bunkhouses.

Camp Orchestra Concerts

Featuring popular classics, swing tunes and original compositions, conducted by Alan Bolt and fellow POWs.

Lectures & Storytelling

Delivered by professors, journalists, engineers and actors among the prisoners, on topics ranging from history to aviation.

Pantomimes & Christmas Shows

Performed entirely by POWs with handmade costumes and props, humorous, chaotic and well-loved.

Books Behind Barbed Wire - The Library at Stalag IV-B

Stalag IV-B had its own, well organised library, which was a vital part of POW life for many prisoners, especially for those who craved mental stimulation or wanted to prepare for life after the war.

In a world of fences, sentries, and hunger, the prison camp library was something quietly remarkable. It didn't look like much, just a section of a wooden hut with shelves made from Red Cross crates, but to many prisoners, it was a lifeline.

Stalag IV-B, like several larger German POW camps, had a functioning library, supplied by the Red Cross, the YMCA, and neutral organisations such as the Swiss Protecting Power. These donations helped stock shelves with a range of books: battered paperbacks, religious texts, detective novels, biographies, encyclopaedias, and language dictionaries. Some were in English, others in French, Russian, or Polish. In a camp that held more than 30,000 men from all over the world, the demand was constant.

The library was run by POWs themselves, often a former schoolteacher or clerk. Borrowing was regulated and orderly. There were handwritten catalogues, lending records and "quiet hours" set aside for study or reading. Prisoners would queue patiently to check out books, sometimes waiting weeks for a popular title to return.

For many, reading was not a pastime but a survival strategy. In their huts, men read to keep their minds sharp and their thoughts elsewhere. One prisoner later wrote, "It was not the barbed wire that was hardest to endure, it was the idleness."

The library helped counter that. Inmates used it to study languages, mathematics, law, or mechanics, often teaching each other in informal groups. Some pursued formal qualifications through correspondence with universities back home. The University of London External Programme even allowed POWs in camps like IV-B to sit recognised exams by post, under guard. It was a remarkable example of human dignity asserting itself under pressure. Albert and Lindsay would have certainly seen the beneficial effects of the library on fellow prisoners and no doubt enjoyed this access to reading materials themselves.

Alongside books, the library often had camp newsletters, mimeographed newspapers (like The Scotsman), and study materials prepared by fellow prisoners.

Some prisoners compiled their own study notes, dictionaries, or even original writings, some of which survive in archives today. (As you read on, you'll see many examples of original work in this book.)

Books circulated endlessly. A volume of Winston Churchill's speeches might pass through twenty hands in a month. These speeches, first published in 1941 as *Into Battle* and followed by later volumes such as *The Unrelenting Struggle* (1942) and *The End of the Beginning* (1943), were widely admired by prisoners. Copies were sometimes included in Red Cross parcels and became prized items in camp libraries. For many POWs, Churchill's voice—captured on the page—offered both courage and a connection to the outside world. In a place designed to suppress identity, his words reminded them of who they were fighting for.

Tattered crime novels were read aloud in groups. Some prisoners began writing their own works, memoirs, poetry, even fictional stories set far from the mud and wire.

Like the football matches and variety shows elsewhere in the camp, the library was more than entertainment. It was a tool for mental resilience. Where theatre brought laughter and football brought release, reading offered reflection. All three provided different ways for POWs to maintain identity, discipline, and a flicker of control over their lives.

What did POWs Read in Stalag IV-B?

- Donated books from the YMCA and Red Cross, including novels, Bibles, and practical manuals

- Language books and dictionaries in French, German, Polish, Russian, Spanish

- Mystery novels by Agatha Christie, John Buchan, and other popular authors

- Political and historical texts, including Winston

Churchill's wartime speeches (e.g. *Into Battle*, 1941)

- Self-made textbooks compiled by prisoners from memory
- Camp newspapers like The Scotsman, produced by the POWs themselves
- Occasional smuggled periodicals or leaflets, depending on camp inspection.

Craftwork and Camp Life

Amid the routine of camp life, many POWs turned to craftwork — not just to pass the time, but to reclaim a sense of purpose. Using salvaged materials like Red Cross tins, wire, string, and wood, men made everything from playing cards and chess sets to model ships, candles, embroidery, carved figurines, and makeshift tools. A few crafted gifts for friends or tokens for loved ones.

This quiet creativity in a world where almost everything had been taken from them and the ability to shape and make something, however small, gave prisoners a sense of control, beauty, and identity.

Though Albert never mentioned it directly, many men in his hut likely whittled or stitched in the evenings. These modest creations were more than hobbies; they were acts of defiance, endurance and hope.

Faith Behind the Wire

On 26th December 1944, Albert Walton sat down in Stalag IV-B to write home. In careful, censored lines, he offered reassurance to his wife Lily, in a world turned upside down:

"I went to church on Christmas Eve and prayed for your safety. We had a good time on Xmas Day and made ourselves quite a feed and at night we had some entertainments."

Simple though it sounds, this quiet sentence says everything. It tells us that even in captivity, even with war still raging and the outcome uncertain, Albert sought comfort, routine and spiritual connection. He wasn't alone. For thousands of men held behind barbed wire, faith offered a vital sense of structure, solace, and dignity.

Makeshift Sanctuaries

There were no stone chapels in Stalag IV-B, but that didn't mean there was no church. A wooden hut served as a multi-denominational space for worship, where services were held when weather, guard routines and resources allowed. Protestant, Catholic, Orthodox and other traditions coexisted respectfully. The services were simple but meaningful: candles fashioned from bacon grease and string, hymn sheets copied out by hand, and crosses carved from salvaged wood.

These services became especially important at times like Christmas. In 1944, the camp was overcrowded and the war was at its bleakest. But that Christmas Eve, Albert, along with hundreds of others, attended a service. In the flicker of handmade candles and the sound of softly sung carols, the men found something of home.

Chaplains and Community

Military chaplains, themselves prisoners, led many of the services. They worked under difficult conditions to conduct sermons, offer pastoral care, and arrange funeral services for those who died in the camp. These chaplains were sustained by YMCA and Red Cross support, which provided religious materials, Bibles, and sacramental items when possible.

The presence of chaplains helped many prisoners, especially at moments when morale was low. Services gave men a place to grieve, reflect, and find hope. It wasn't about religion for everyone; some men came for the quiet, for the hymns, or simply to feel human for an hour.

Unity and Meaning

Albert never spoke much about his time as a POW, but his words from Christmas 1944 resonate deeply. His decision to attend church and to write about it suggests that it meant something to him. Whether it was a prayer for his family's safety or simply a moment of emotional clarity, faith gave him a place to stand.

Albert's letter went on to describe a shared meal and an evening of entertainment, no doubt with Jock and other friends from their hut, moments that reminded the men of life outside the wire.

Christmas Postcard

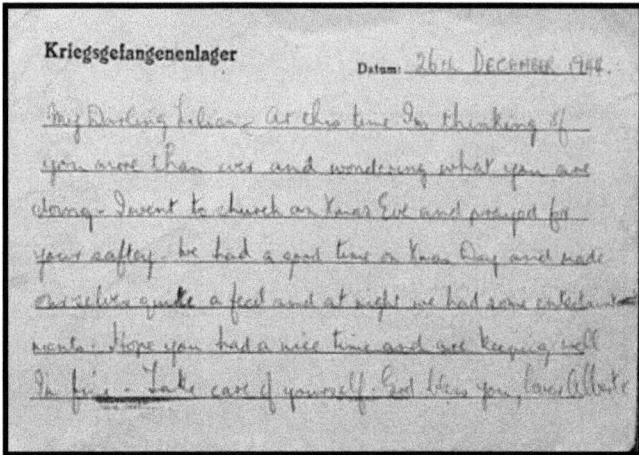

13.1 Letters from captivity

During his time as a prisoner of war, Albert maintained a connection to home through regular letters to his beloved wife, Lilian. Married in 1942, Lilian remained the constant anchor in his life during his long captivity. Albert's letters, carefully written and dutifully sent, were both a lifeline and a testament to his enduring love and concern for her.

While the contents of the letters might seem mundane to an outsider, they reveal much about Albert's character. He often asked about Lilian's welfare, focusing on practical concerns such as whether she was receiving the correct financial allowances, likely a dependents' allowance provided to the families of servicemen. Ever meticulous and shrewd with money, Albert didn't want his family to go without during his absence.

Postcard Written 24th May 1944

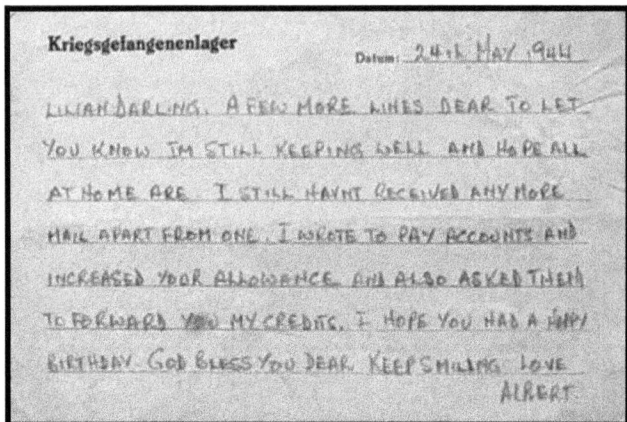

He also wrote about Red Cross parcels, socks and other simple details of daily life, keeping the tone optimistic despite the bleakness of his situation. The absence of deeper emotional reflection may have been partly due to the strict censorship, but it also reflected Albert's intent to shield Lilian from unnecessary worry.

Albert's sister Anne recalled how his letters used to sometimes contain coded messages. 'There was one letter where Albert wrote "tell Alfie Wilson they are treating us well"…. and Alfie did not exist, so from that, we were able to piece together the coded message that Albert was actually having a terrible time.'

Postcard Written 26th September 1944

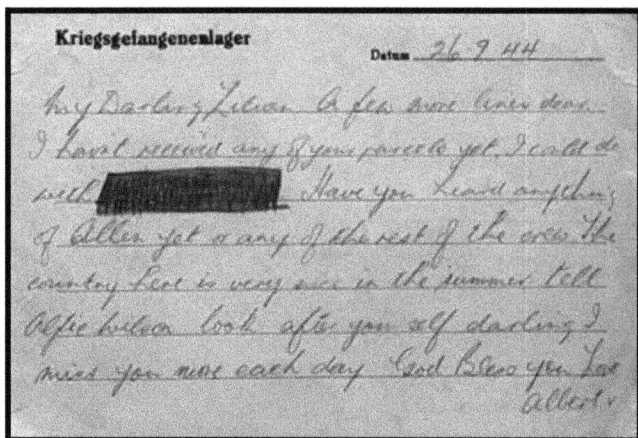

It's heartbreaking to read that Albert is still regularly enquiring after Alan Lazenby and the rest of the crew.

Albert's family recalls a small suitcase stored in their home, filled with these cherished letters. Written on thin, slightly glazed paper, each sheet was pre-printed with sections to be completed, folding into its own envelope for easy mailing. The letters were meticulously handwritten, though interspersed with holes where words had been burnt out with a lit cigarette; a stark reminder of the censoring process POW correspondence endured.

Sadly, the fate of the suitcase filled with these letters remains unknown. However, we're so pleased to have 21 postcards written by Albert and sent to Lily throughout 1944, which are carefully preserved within the family. To read them now provides a remarkable window into Albert's life during his time as a prisoner, a poignant blend of the mundane, the practical, and the deeply human connection he shared with his wife. These letters were a thread of hope and normality during a time of immense uncertainty, carrying his love across the miles and behind enemy lines.

The psychological toll of captivity was immense. Disease and malnutrition were constant battles, and the mental strain of confinement led some men to take their own lives. There were also harrowing accounts of British Servicemen burying their comrades after German guards executed escape attempts.

When ultimately liberated by the Red Army on 23rd April, 1945, the camp's grim legacy was undeniable. It is estimated that around 3,000 internees had perished due to illness and the dire living conditions. The fallen were buried in a cemetery in Neuburxdorf, where a memorial now stands to honour all the lives lost within the camp's confines.

Stalag IV-B remains a stark reminder of the cruelty of war, yet also of the resilience and ingenuity of those who endured it. Despite the deprivations and despair, the prisoners' efforts to sustain morale through creative expression and communal solidarity offer a poignant testament to the human spirit under the most challenging of circumstances.

CHAPTER 14

A Glimmer of Triumph Amid Captivity

A mid the monotony and hardship of Albert Walton's captivity in 1944, two remarkable milestones brought a sense of pride and accomplishment to the Walton family.

The first came in April 1944, when Albert was awarded a Good Conduct Badge to commemorate four years of service in the RAF. The badge, a simple yet meaningful recognition, symbolised loyalty, discipline, and steadfastness. Although confined within the barbed wire of Stalag IV-B, the presentation of this award would have been a rare moment of formality and camaraderie. Inmates likely made the most of the occasion, gathering as the badge was presented in a small, improvised ceremony. For Albert, it must have been a bittersweet reminder of his life as an airman, a life that had been abruptly interrupted. The badge would have been worn with quiet pride, a token of his perseverance even in captivity.

While Albert celebrated this achievement behind enemy lines, the Walton family had reason to rejoice back home. In June 1944, news reached West Boldon that Albert's father, Alexander Walton, had been named in the King's Birthday Honours List and awarded the British Empire Medal (BEM) for meritorious service in the Merchant Navy.

The story made the local newspaper, The Shields Gazette on Monday, 11th June, 1944:

"West Boldon Man's B.E.M.: Sea Service

The award of the British Empire Medal (Civil Division) has been received by Mr Alexander Walton of 10 Addison Road, West Boldon, for meritorious service at sea whilst serving in the Merchant Navy.

This information was received by Mr Walton from the Director General of the Ministry of War Transport.

Aged 58 years, Mr Walton has served with the Merchant Navy for 43 years and at the time of the award he was Boatswain. He was torpedoed on two occasions during the last war [WW1], and has also been torpedoed three times during the present war [WW2]. On the last occasion he received severe bodily injuries and has been since discharged from the service.

Mr Walton lost his eldest son in the Royal Navy over a year ago, has a son a prisoner of war, another son in the Navy, and a daughter serving in the Women's Auxiliary Police Service.

Mr Walton is now employed by the Bitulac Works at East Boldon."

A Glimmer of Triumph Amid Captivity

The Walton family must have been bursting with pride as Alexander prepared to travel to London to receive his medal from the King at St James's Palace. Photographs taken at the gates of the Palace show Alexander proudly displaying his medal, accompanied by his wife, Caroline, and his daughter, Elwyn, who was serving in the Women's Auxiliary Police Force. Yet the moment was far from simple for Alexander. While he stood at the gates of St James's Palace, his thoughts must have turned to the sacrifices his family had endured during the war.

Alex Walton (BME) photographed outside St James Palace, with wife and daughter

His eldest son, Norman, had been lost in the Royal Navy over a year earlier. Another son, Albert, was a prisoner of war in Germany, enduring unimaginable hardships. Stanley, his third son, was serving in the Royal Navy, navigating the treacherous waters of the war. Even Elwyn, standing beside him at the palace, was contributing to the war effort. Alexander's medal was not just a testament to his own bravery but also a reflection of the resilience and sacrifice of his entire family.

Family accounts provide a fuller picture of the extraordinary circumstances that led to Alexander's medal. During the war, while serving in the Merchant Navy as a boatswain, his ship was torpedoed—a grim ordeal that left him with serious leg injuries. Despite his wounds, Alexander stayed aboard the stricken vessel to aid a fellow crew member. The rest of the surviving crew evacuated in a lifeboat, but the enemy targeted and sank it, killing everyone aboard. Alexander and his injured crewmate were able to later board a life raft and were left clinging to it for their lives over several days as they drifted in the frigid waters before being rescued.

It is believed that the specifics of Alexander's bravery were omitted from the official citation—a practice during wartime, possibly for security reasons—but the story passed through generations of the Walton family as a testament to his courage and sacrifice.

Throughout the Second World War, the Merchant Navy played a critical but often underappreciated role in sustaining the war effort. Merchant seamen kept Britain supplied with essential food, fuel, and military equipment, braving the treacherous Atlantic and Arctic waters under constant threat from German U-boats, aircraft, and surface raiders.

Their convoys, often lightly armed and vulnerable, were lifelines that ensured factories could keep producing, troops could be equipped, and civilians could survive. The Arctic convoys, in particular, faced not only enemy attacks but also brutal weather conditions as they carried vital supplies to the Soviet Union, helping to keep the Eastern Front alive.

The risks faced by the Merchant Navy were staggering. More than 30,000 merchant seamen lost their lives during the war, a casualty rate proportionally higher than that of the Royal Navy or any of the armed forces. Many went down with their ships, torpedoed far from rescue, while others endured the horrors of lifeboat survival in freezing seas. Despite the dangers, these civilian sailors continued to crew the convoys, often returning to sea as soon as they reached port. Their courage and strength underpinned the war effort, ensuring that Britain and its allies remained supplied, even during the darkest days of the Battle of the Atlantic.

Back in captivity, Albert learned of his father's award through letters from Caroline and his beloved wife, Lilian. In a world so removed from his family's celebrations, this news must have been a rare moment of joy and pride and a reminder of the strength and resilience that ran through the Walton family.

Postcard Written on 10th October 1944

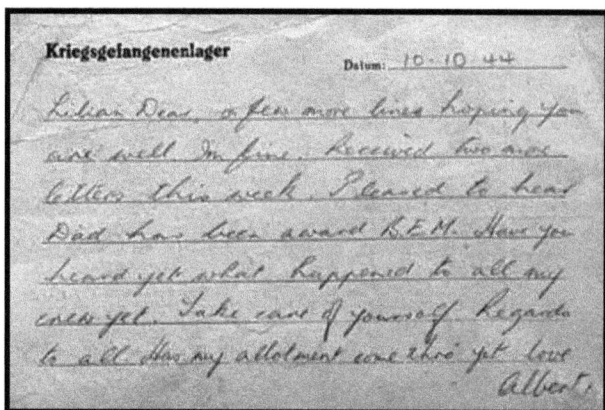

While Albert's active service was curtailed, his brother Stan was fighting on behalf of the whole Walton family.

Family at War

Stanley Walton, Albert's younger brother, born on 11th January, 1926, in South Shields, served as a Signalman in the Royal Navy during World War II, his service number PJ-114968 marking his record of duty. Although official details of his service remain sparse, his son Brian Walton has preserved vivid memories that offer insight into his experiences at sea.

As a Signalman, Stanley's responsibilities were critical to the success of anti-submarine operations. He managed both visual communications—using signal flags and sema-phore—and electronic transmissions via radio, ensuring that messages were relayed accurately during convoy oper-ations. In an era when the threat from German U-boats loomed large over Allied shipping lanes, Stanley's role helped coordinate manoeuvres and maintain fleet cohesion under the constant pressure of enemy attack.

Stanley in his "No 10 Dress" uniform, denoting the picture was taken in a hot climate.

His son Brian recalls a particularly memorable tradition from his father's time at sea. Every time the crew set sail, a rousing version of "A-Hunting We Will Go" would echo over the loudspeakers. This stirring song, associated with the aggressive anti-submarine tactics championed by Captain "Johnnie" Walker, became the signature tune for Stanley's team. While it is not definitively confirmed that Stanley served directly in Walker's fleet, the adoption of this anthem suggests that his crew embraced a similar combative spirit, using the song to boost morale and signal their intent to hunt and destroy German U-boats.

For Stanley and his comrades, the success of each mission depended on precise, unwavering communication, an effort that often went unsung but was essential to the protection of Allied convoys. His work as a signalman contributed significantly to the broader war effort, ensuring that critical information flowed seamlessly between ships in the dangerous waters of the Atlantic.

Stanley Walton's service stands as a testament to the vital, if often understated, role of signalmen in World War II. The memory of that iconic song and the proud, determined spirit of his crew continue to echo in the family's recollections, a reminder of a time when even the smallest role could be the difference between peril and survival. He remained in service with the Royal Navy after WWII right up until 1950.

14.1 Captivity in Stalag Luft III Belaria: The Parallel Story of Craig and McClure

While Albert and his colleague, Sergeant Charles Lindsay, endured their imprisonment in Stalag IV-B, two other crew members from their Lancaster, Flying Officer Weston Craig and Flying Officer James McClure, found themselves confined in a different camp: Stalag Luft III Belaria.

Unlike Stalag IV-B, which housed a mix of Servicemen from various Allied forces, Stalag Luft III was specifically built for captured airmen officers. Despite being held separately from Albert and Lindsay, Craig and McClure were fortunate to be placed in the same hut, alongside ten other prisoners from different corners of the world.

Original Lancaster Bomber Sketch by John Battle, a fellow inmate of McClure and Craig at Stalag Luft III

What set Stalag Luft III apart was not only its notorious role in The Great Escape but also the unique bond formed among the airmen. The shared experience of captivity fostered a deep sense of camaraderie, and, in the face of hardship, the men found ways to support one another.

James McClure: The Sketching Storyteller

Among those confined within the barbed-wire enclosure of Stalag Luft III, F/O James McClure stood out for his talent in writing and sketching. Like many POWs, he kept a journal, chronicling daily life and capturing the essence of imprisonment through detailed illustrations. His journal provides us with a rare, firsthand account of the conditions inside the camp, a window into the struggles, routines and small victories that defined their existence.

Stalag Luft III Sketch by FO James McClure, 1944

One of McClure's most notable contributions is a bird's-eye view map of Stalag Luft III, a testament to his keen observation skills and artistic precision. His sketches document not only the camp's layout but also the way prisoners organised their lives within it. The huts, the roll-call areas, the mess hall, the guards' patrol routes – each line on the map tells a story of resilience, survival, and the constant yearning for freedom.

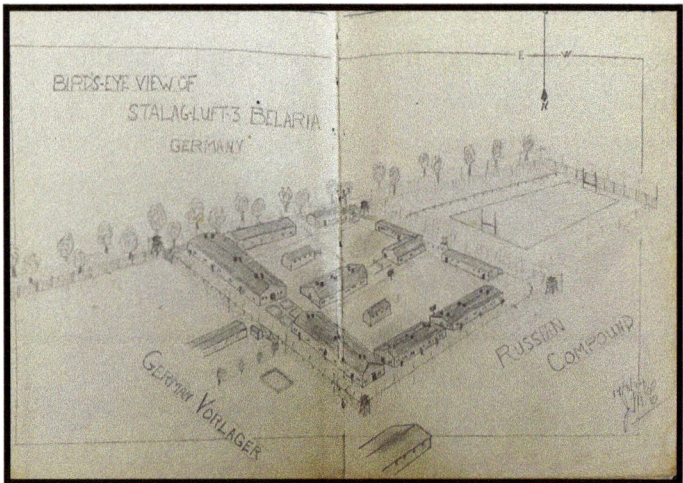

The Harsh Realities of POW Life

Life in Stalag Luft III Belaria mirrored much of what Albert and Lindsay experienced in Stalag IV-B. The daily routines were rigidly enforced by their captors:

- Morning roll call in the freezing cold, where guards counted every prisoner, ensuring none had escaped overnight.

- Meagre rations distributed in the mess hall, barely sufficient to sustain the men.

- Forced labour for some prisoners, though airmen were usually exempt under the Geneva Convention.

- Endless hours of waiting... waiting for news, for letters from home, for the war to end.

Perhaps the greatest challenge of all was hunger. Food was painfully scarce, and German rations were inadequate to meet even the most basic nutritional needs. Each prisoner received a measly allowance of:

- A small loaf of black bread, often stale and barely edible.
- Watery soup, sometimes flavoured with a hint of turnip or cabbage.
- Occasionally, a portion of sausage or margarine, though never enough.

FOOD

(GERMAN ISSUE FOR ONE WEEK)

5 OUNCES SUGAR	2 OZS CHEESE
2 OUNCES JAM	2 OZS FRESH MEAT
1 LOAF BLACK BREAD	1 OZ BLOOD SAUSAGE
7 OZS MARGARINE	ACORN COFFEE (OCCASIONALLY)
30 POTATOES	SALT
TURNIPS, SWEDES OR CABBAGE	DRIED VEG (OCCASIONALLY)
3 CUPS BARLEY (COOKED)	

(GERMAN ISSUED UTENSILS)

TO EACH MAN	TO THE ROOM
1 FORK	1 KEIN TRINKWASSER
1 KNIFE	1 PORCELAIN JUG
1 SPOON	1 BASIN
1 CUP	
1 BOWL	

The real lifeline for prisoners came in the form of Red Cross parcels, which, when they arrived, were a godsend. These parcels contained essentials such as powdered milk, canned meat, biscuits, tea, coffee, and chocolate—treasures that were often rationed and shared among the men. When Red Cross supplies were delayed or stolen by guards, hunger set in and morale plummeted.

RED CROSS

ONCE PER WEEK, SUPPLIES PERMITTING, EACH P.O.W. WAS ISSUED ONE RED CROSS FOOD PARCEL - BRITISH, CANADIAN, AMERICAN OR NEW ZEALAND.

BRITISH		CANADIAN		AMERICAN		NEW ZEALAND	
MEAT + VEG	1 TIN	CORNED BEEF	1 TIN	CORNED BEEF	1 TIN	BEEF	1 TIN
MEAT ROLL	1 TIN	SPAM	1 TIN	SPAM	1 TIN	TONGUE	1 TIN
BISCUITS	1 TIN	BISCUITS	1 LARGE PKT	BISCUITS	1 BOX	CHEESE	8 OZ
CHEESE	3 OZS	CHEESE	4 OZS	CHEESE	8 OZS	CONDENSED MILK	1 TIN
CONDENSED MILK	1 TIN	KLIM	1 TIN	POWDERED MILK	1 TIN	SUGAR	8 OZ
SUGAR	4 OZS	SUGAR	7 OZS	MARGARINE	1 LB	HONEY	12 OZ
MARGARINE	8 OZS	BUTTER	1 LB	SUGAR	8 OZS	TEA	4 OZ
JAM	8 OZS	JAM	1 LB	MEAT PATÉ	1 TIN	BUTTER	1 LB
SALMON	1 TIN	PRUNES	3 OZS	PRUNES	1 LB	CAFÉ AU LAIT	1 T
TEA	2 OZS	RAISINS	7 OZS	SALMON	1 TIN	DRIED PEAS	1 P
COCOA	4 OZS	SALMON	1 TIN	SARDINES	1 TIN	CHOCOLATE	8 O
CHOCOLATE	4 OZS	SARDINES	1 TIN	NESCAFE	1 TIN		
SOAP	1 BAR	COFFEE	6 OZS	ORANGE CRYSTALS	2 PACKETS		
		CHOCOLATE	5 OZS	CHOCOLATE	8 OZS		
		SALT	1 OZ	SOAP	2 BARS		
		SOAP	1 BAR	CIGARETTES	100		

The Great Escape and Its Aftermath

Stalag Luft III was infamous for its elaborate tunnelling operations, and it was from this very camp that The Great Escape took place in March 1944. The prisoners had spent many months (over a year) digging three tunnels—Tom, Dick, and Harry—and meticulously planning their breakout. When the escape finally happened, 76 men managed to flee, only to be relentlessly hunted down. In a brutal act of retribution, 47 of the escapees were executed by the Gestapo on Hitler's orders.

The news of the executions sent shockwaves through the camp. The remaining prisoners, including Craig and McClure, were devastated but also defiant. A memorial service was held on 13th April 1944 in honour of the 47 officers who were executed, a solemn and deeply moving ceremony that reinforced the prisoners' unity in the face of tyranny. James McClure recorded the ceremonial proceedings in his journal below.

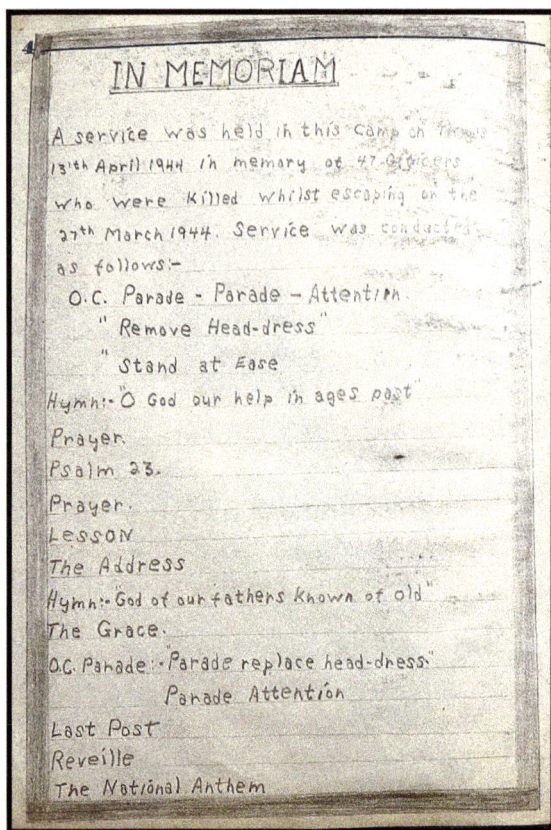

IN MEMORIAM

A service was held in this Camp on the 13th April 1944 in memory of 47 Officers who were killed whilst escaping on the 27th March 1944. Service was conducted as follows:-

O.C. Parade - Parade - Attention.
   " Remove Head-dress"
   " Stand at Ease"
Hymn: "O God our help in ages past"
Prayer.
Psalm 23.
Prayer.
Lesson
The Address
Hymn:- "God of our fathers known of old"
The Grace.
O.C. Parade - "Parade replace head-dress"
        Parade Attention
Last Post
Reveille
The National Anthem

The memorial service at Stalag Luft III Belaria was unlike anything the prisoners had ever experienced. As they stood in solemn ranks, the weight of what had happened pressed heavily upon them. The execution of 47 recaptured escapees was not just a tragedy: it was an atrocity. These men had not been criminals; they had simply followed their duty as officers, bound by the unspoken code that every prisoner of war must try to escape. And for that, they had been executed.

McClure, ever the observer, recorded the details of the service in his journal. Through his words, we can vividly picture the scene: a gathering of men, battle-hardened yet hollow-eyed, their grief raw. The officers leading the service spoke with quiet dignity, their voices steady despite the sorrow that gripped them all.

There was pride, too. Pride in what had been attempted, in the brilliance and determination that had gone into planning the escape. The tunnels had been dug with painstaking precision, the disguises crafted with ingenuity, the forgeries executed with a skill that rivalled the finest counterfeiters. It had been a masterful operation, one that should have ended in freedom, not slaughter.

Yet, beneath that pride was a deep and abiding sorrow. Some men bowed their heads, unable to meet the eyes of their comrades. Others stood rigid, fists clenched at their sides. And for many, the simple act of breathing felt heavier than it had the day before. The Germans had carried out their executions without mercy, disregarding the rules of war and every man standing there knew it. The injustice of it all was suffocating.

Was there a dry eye to be found? Unlikely. As the final notes of The Last Post rang out, followed by the stark clarity of Reveille, the weight of the moment became unbearable. Then came the solemn strains of The National Anthem, a final act of defiance, a reassurance that their fallen comrades would not be forgotten. The tears must have fallen then, silent and unbidden. These were strong men, men who had endured months or years of captivity, men who had faced down enemy fire in the skies over Europe. But this? This was different. The sheer brutality of it cut deeper than any physical wound. It was not just the loss of friends, but the crushing reminder of their own helplessness.

In the days that followed, the camp felt changed. The usual murmurs of laughter, the clatter of makeshift games, even the distant strains of a harmonica—all of it faded into a heavy silence. Morale had taken a devastating blow. The war carried on, but for those left behind at Stalag Luft III, something had shifted. The Great Escape had been the largest breakout attempt of the war, a symbol of defiance and determination. Now, it was marked by grief, by anger, and by an unshakable sense of loss.

Through McClure's journal, we glimpse this moment as it truly was—not just a historical event, but a deeply human one. It allows us to stand beside them in that quiet, grief-stricken crowd, to feel the sting of injustice, the weight of remembrance, and the aching absence of those who should have been standing there too.

Little acts of defiance surfaced in the wake of this atrocity. Some prisoners sketched satirical cartoons mocking their captors, while others composed poetry that hinted at their thirst for justice when the war was over. McClure himself contributed to this quiet resistance, capturing the mood in his artwork and journal entries.

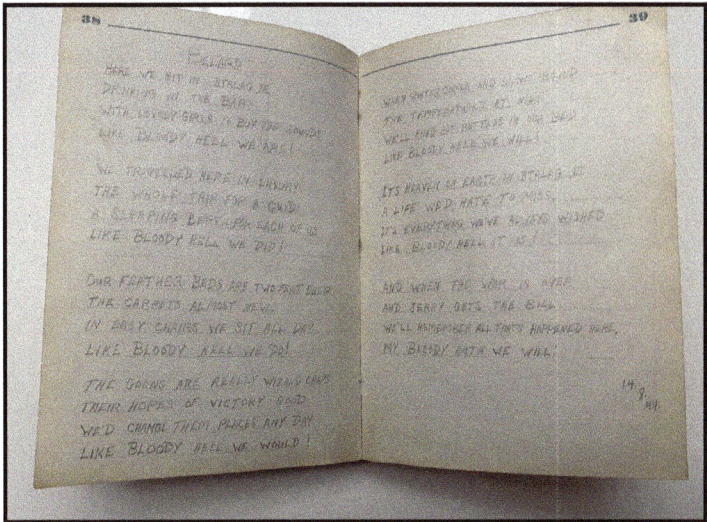

BELARIA - Poem by James McClure

Here We Sit In Stalag III
Drinking In The Bar
With Lovely Girls To Buy The Rounds
Like Bloody Hell We Are!

We Travelled Here In Luxury
The Whole Trip For A Quid
A Sleeping Berth For Each Of Us
Like Bloody Hell We Did!

Our Feather Beds Are Two Feet Deep
The Carpets Almost New
In Easy Chairs We Sit All Day
Like Bloody Hell We Do!

The Goons Are Really Wizard Chaps
Their Hopes Of Victory Good
We'd Change Them Places Any Day
Like Bloody Hell We Would!

When Winter Comes And Snows Abound
The Temperature's At Nil
We'll Find Hot Bottles In Our Bed
Like Bloody Hell We Will!

It's Heaven On Earth In Stalag III
A Life We'd Hate To Miss,
It's Everything We've Always Wished
Like Bloody Hell It Is!

And When The War Is Over
And Jerry Gets The Bill
We'll Remember All That's Happened Here,
My Bloody Oath We Will!

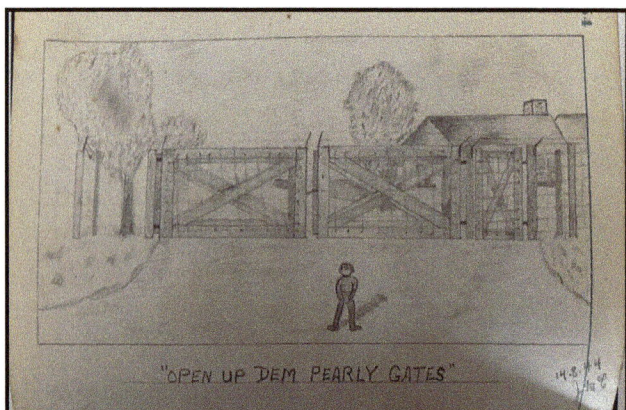

"OPEN UP DEM PEARLY GATES"

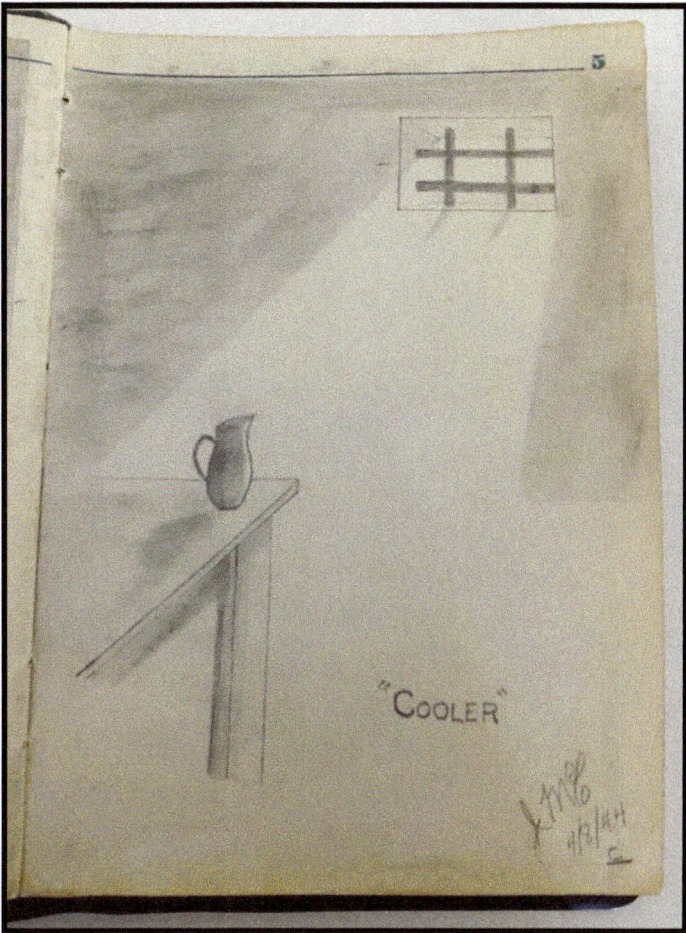

"Cooler"

A Brotherhood Formed in Captivity

Despite the grim conditions, the men in Craig and McClure's hut developed a strong brotherhood, bound by their shared ordeal. They became a tightly knit group, offering one another support, companionship, and humour to survive the long months of captivity.

23

SMILE - YOU SINNER SMILE

NEVER LOSE THAT GOLDEN GIFT
OF LAUGHTER AND A SMILE
YOUR CAPTORS HAVE THE UPPER HAND
BUT ONLY FOR A WHILE.

DEEP WITHIN YOUR STALWART HEART
KEEP THE FLAME OF HOPE AWAKE
YOUR BODY, MAYBE THEY CONFINE
BUT YOUR SPIRIT THEY CANT BREAK.

THINGS ARE BOUND TO TURN OUT RIGHT
AND SUNSHINE YOU CAN FIND
IF YOUR THOUGHTS DWELL ON YOUR LOVED ONES
IN THE LAND YOU LEFT BEHIND.

SO DONT FORGET TO TAKE THAT SMILE
AND LAUGHTER HOME WITH YOU
AFTER ALL YOUR FOLKS ANXIETY
ITS THE LEAST THAT YOU CAN DO.

FOR. IT SHOWS FOLKS THAT IN SPITE OF ALL
YOU MAY SUFFER AND ENDURE
YOUR A MAN WHOSE STERLING MANLINESS
STOOD THE ACRID TEST OF WAR.

COPIED FROM BOOK OF
ARCHIE GALLOWAY

With so much time on their hands, the men turned to various pastimes:

- Sketching and Writing – Many, like McClure, documented their experiences through art and words.

- Gardening – Though limited, some prisoners managed to cultivate small patches of vegetables, a rare luxury.

- Cooking – A strange but common activity, prisoners often imagined recipes they would cook once free. Some even attempted to improvise meals using Red Cross supplies.

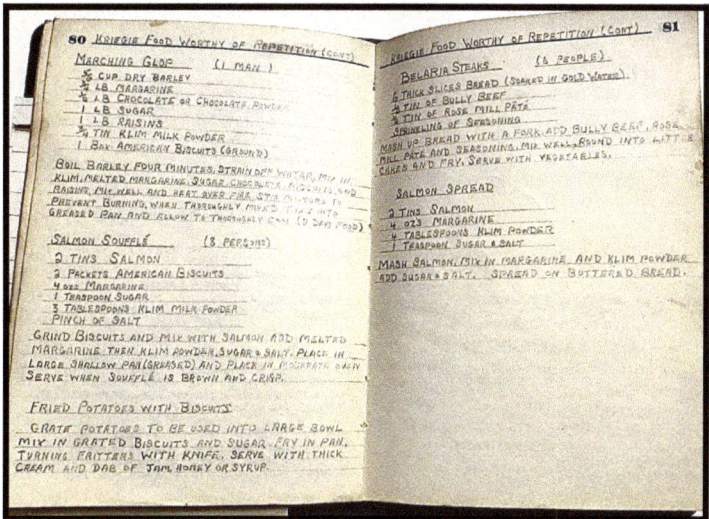

With time, the men observed each other's quirks and personalities, leading to friendly mockery and inside jokes. One of the most humorous and insightful expressions of this camaraderie came from Weston Craig and Dennis Perrin, who wrote a light-hearted poem about their inmates.

Weston Craig & Dennis Perrins's Poetic Skit

Written with his fellow hut mate Dennis Perrin, no doubt

as a bit of fun intended to put a smile on the faces of other inmates, this is a brilliant piece of characterisation. Zimmer Fünfzehn translates to Room Fifteen.

11

ZIMMER FÜNFZEHN

I'll tell you the tale of Belaria,
For there's lots you ought to know,
Of the gallant chaps who lived there
What a pity they all had to go.

Chief in the room was a "Squaddie,"
But to us he was just known as Ted;
His one great talent was belching,
Doubtless due to the way he was fed.

An angular type was Paul Barber,
Who stood rather tall in his socks;
He tripped round the room like a fairy,
And littered the floor with cracked crocks.

Playfair perversely called "Tiny,"
Was wont to lodge in our room;
He spent most of his time getting sun-tanned,
And foretelling our imminent doom.

There was also a Welshman called Battle,
Who was always most willing to shirk;
He said that his best friend was Totty—
He said that his worst friend was work!

(Continued overleaf)

ZIMMER FUNFZEHN CONTINUED

A colliery lad was our Norman,
A Hetton type both born and bred;
No matter what brew we demanded,
He gave us iced coffee instead,

An aged old veteran was Stanley,
A disciple of Charlie Bedaux;
Although he hadn't been down long,
'What's the difference' he wanted to know.

Our Jim was a true blood Canadian,
His statistical speech made us quail;
He said that all men were born equal,
But he hogged all the parcels and mail.

The senior wop was old Reeder
Whose boast was the women he'd caught;
He was forced to mark time in an Oflag,
But the future looked wizard he thought.

A product of Glasgow was Archie,
A principled lad — so he said;
No matter just what the discussion
"I'm agin it" was heard from his bed.

(continued overleaf)

ZIMMER FUNFZEHN CONTINUED

Owd Bob was a native of Yorkshire,
For his appetite famed far and wide,
Before every meal he hunted for crusts,
To fill his voracious inside.

Last but not least are the authors,
Dennis and Weston, to wit,
So fond of ourselves, and quite rightly,
That we just dont belong to this skit.

ZIMMER FÜNFZEHN

I'll tell you the tale of Belaría.
For there's lots you ought to know,
Of the gallant chaps who lived there
What a pity they all had to go.

Chiet in the room was a "Squaddie,"
But to us he was just known as Ted;
His one great talent was belching,
Doubtless due to the way he was fed.

An angular type was Paul Barber,
Who Stood rather tall in his socks;
He tripped round the room like a fairy,
And littered the floor with cracked crocks.

Playfair perversely called "Tiny".
Was wont to lodge in our room;
He spent most of his time getting sun-tanned,
And foretelling our imminent doom.

There was also a Welshman called Battle,
Who was always most willing to shirk;
He said that his best friend was Totty-
He said that his worst friend was work!

A colliery lad was our Norman,
A Hetton type both born and bred;
No matter what brew we demanded,
He gave us iced coffee, instead,

An aged old veteran was Stanley.
A disciple of Charlie Bedaux;
Although he hadn't been down long.
"What's the difference" he wanted to know.

Our Jim was a true blood Canadian,
His statistical speech made us quail;
He said that all men were born equal,
But he hogged all the parcels and mail.

The senior WOP was old Reeder
Whose boast was the women he'd caught:
He was forced to mark time in an Oflag.
But the future looked wizard he thought.

A product of Glasgow was Archie,
A principled lad – so he said;
No matter just what the discussion
"Im agin it" was heard from his bed

Ord Bob was a native of Yorkshire,
For his appetite famed far and wide,
Before every meal he hunted for crusts,
To fill his voracious inside.

Last but not least are the authors,
Dennis and Weston, to wit.
So fond of ourselves, and quite rightly.
That we just don't belong to this skit.

Craig's poem provided an amusing take on the unique traits of each man in the hut, a morale booster that brought laughter in dark times. One particularly memorable line describes James McClure:

"His statistical speech made us quail."

McClure's daughter Brenda later explained the meaning behind this: he was a man for facts and figures, known for his precise, logical mind. Whether discussing camp rations, the likelihood of an escape plan succeeding, or debating the war's progress, McClure had a habit of breaking things down into carefully calculated details.

The Christmas Menu 1944

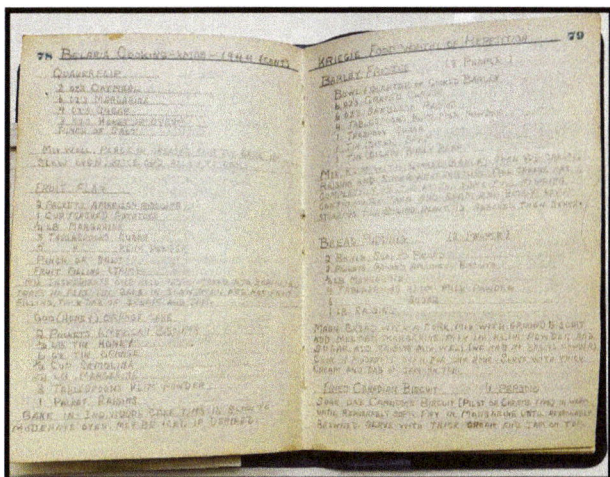

A Brother's Compassionate Mission

During James McClure's imprisonment, his brother, Hank McClure, also an RCAF serviceman stationed in England, learned of the air crash involving his brother's crew and the casualties it incurred. Demonstrating profound empathy, Hank sought to convey condolences personally to a family affected by the tragedy.

Visit to the Lazenby Family in Scarborough

Among those who perished was F/L Alan Lazenby, the pilot of flight DV269, whose family resided in Scarborough. Hank visited the Lazenby household to offer his sympathies, possibly delivering messages from his brother James to the grieving family. This gesture of solidarity amidst shared sorrow exemplifies the deep bonds formed among those enduring the hardships of war.

An Unexpected Meeting and Blossoming Romance

During his visit to Scarborough, Hank met Myra Craven, a close friend of the Lazenby family. Their encounter, rooted in the sombre context of loss, gradually blossomed into a profound connection. Despite the surrounding turmoil, Hank and Myra's relationship flourished, leading to their later marriage.

New Beginnings in Winnipeg

Following their union, Myra relocated to Winnipeg, Canada, where the couple established their life together.

Their story shows the capacity for love to emerge even amidst the darkest times.

Legacy of the McClure and Lazenby Connection

The convergence of the McClure and Lazenby families during World War II illustrates the unforeseen ways in which lives intersect during pivotal historical moments. From the tragedy of flight DV269's downing to the enduring love between Hank and Myra, this narrative encapsulates the profound human experiences that arise from the complexities of war.

The Waiting Game and Hope for Liberation

By 1945, the prisoners sensed that the war was nearing its end. Allied forces were closing in and rumours of impending liberation spread like wildfire. Yet, time dragged on painfully, and uncertainty remained; would they be freed, or would the Germans force them on a brutal march deeper into occupied territory?

For Craig, McClure, and the other men in their hut, the only option was to endure, to hold onto hope that soon the barbed wire fences would no longer confine them.

The Long March and Liberation at Stalag III-A, Luckenwalde

As the brutal winter of 1945 gripped Germany, thousands of Allied prisoners of war, including Weston Craig and James McClure, were forced to embark on one of the most gruelling ordeals of their captivity, the infamous Long March.

Evacuation from Stalag Luft III (Belaria) – 28th January, 1945

By early 1945, the war was turning against Germany. The Soviet Red Army was advancing rapidly from the east, pushing deep into German-held territory. In response, the Germans began evacuating POW camps to prevent prisoners from falling into Soviet hands. On 28th January, 1945, the men at Stalag Luft III (Belaria), a subcamp of the famous Stalag Luft III, were roused in the dead of night and ordered to prepare for departure. The temperature was well below freezing, the ground was covered in deep snow, and the men were given little time to gather their meagre belongings.

Under armed guard, the column of ten thousand prisoners began their harrowing march westward through war-torn Germany. There was no transport, no provisions; they trudged through mile after mile of bitterly cold terrain in tattered uniforms and worn-out boots.

The Long March – Hundreds of Kilometres in the Snow

The forced march lasted for days, covering several hundred kilometres through snow-laden fields, forests and bombed-out villages. The men were exhausted, hungry, and physically drained, yet they had no choice but to keep moving. Nights were spent in barns, abandoned buildings, or out in the open, with whatever scraps of straw they could find for warmth. Food was scarce and many survived on frozen turnips scavenged from fields or the occasional morsel of bread handed out by local farmers.

Frostbite was a constant threat, and illness ran rampant among the prisoners. Some men simply could not go on, collapsing in the snow and succumbing to the bitter cold. Those who fell behind were at the mercy of the guards. Some were left to die, while others were shot as an example to keep the column moving.

Through sheer willpower, Weston Craig, James McClure, and their fellow prisoners endured this week-long ordeal, finally arriving at their destination: Stalag III-A, Luckenwalde, on 4th February, 1945.

Imprisonment at Stalag III-A, Luckenwalde

Stalag III-A, located 50 kilometres south of Berlin, was a massive POW camp originally built to house Polish prisoners in 1939. By 1945, it was severely overcrowded, holding thousands of men from across the Allied nations.

The conditions at Luckenwalde were dire. The camp was infested with lice, food rations were minimal, and medical supplies were nearly non-existent. The men were physically drained from the march, their bodies weakened by hunger, frostbite and exhaustion. Despite this, they clung to hope, knowing the war was nearing its end.

14.2   The Weight of War

The latter half of 1944 was a period marked by hardship, hope and secret acts of defiance for Albert and his family.

At Stalag IV-B:

The camp was overcrowded, sanitation was abysmal, and food was scarce. Such conditions led to widespread malnutrition, lice infestation, and disease. Albert did later divulge to family that he'd been so starving, he'd eaten the wood slats from his bed and insects and worms from around the camp. However, in his letters, he does say he's eating well, possibly so as not to worry anyone, or perhaps because prisoners were forced to say that. One theme that kept appearing in his letters was no parcels from home yet and cigarettes in short supply (25 per week).

Postcard Written on 3rd October 1944

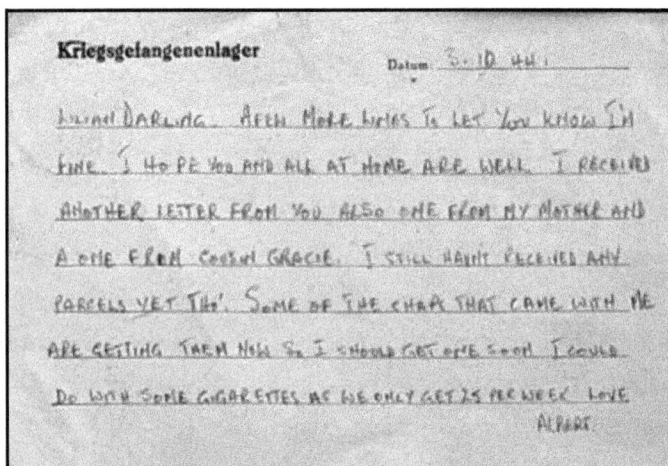

Even within this bleak environment, there were sparks of rebellion and ingenuity. Rumours circulated among the prisoners about secret tunnelling activities. In whispered conversations late at night, men spoke of digging escape tunnels beneath the barbed wire. Some daring groups even organised clandestine efforts to dig their way out, hoping to find a route to freedom. Although many of these attempts were thwarted by vigilant guards and the ever-present threat of discovery, the mere act of tunnelling was an act of defiance, showing a belief that freedom might be just one shovelful of earth away.

On the Home Front – Lily's Hope

Back in England, life on the home front was no less challenging. Lily worked long hours in a munitions factory; a vital but gruelling job that kept the war effort supplied. With rationing in full swing and grim news from every quarter, hope was a precious commodity. Desperate for reassurance amid the uncertainty, Lily sought solace in an unlikely place, a fortune teller. In a small, dimly lit room, the seer predicted that Albert would return safely and that, in time, they would build a family together. This prophecy became a cherished beacon of hope for Lily. Though the odds were slim and the future uncertain, she clung to those words, finding strength in the belief that love would prevail, and indeed, that vision turned out to be true.

For the Entire Family

Meanwhile, Albert's father, Alex, had recently been discharged from the Merchant Navy due to a severe leg injury sustained during his long service. His discharge marked the end of an era for him yet also added to the family's collective hope that the Allied victory was imminent. Across the country, rationing continued to tighten and the news from the front was often grim. Air raids interrupted sleep most nights. The threats were constant. However, even as another wartime Christmas loomed, a holiday marked by scarcity rather than abundance, the family remained united in their hope for victory.

In every corner of their lives, from the secret tunnels beneath Stalag IV-B to the factory floors, the Walton family and their compatriots found ways to persevere. The hardships of the latter half of 1944 were met with resourcefulness and an enduring belief that brighter days were ahead.

The wartime efforts continued at pace, night after night Bomber Command were causing severe damage behind the German lines, flattening the largest cities and infrastructure. Newspapers across the country gave daily war updates on the gains that were being made, glimmers of hope that Great Britain and the allied nations would succeed against the iron grip of the Nazi. So important was rationing, headlines also included Christmas nut allowances.

Shields Gazette December 1944

Shields Gazette

And Shipping Telegraph. FINAL

FRIDAY, DECEMBER 1, 1944

GENERAL PATTON REACHES SAAR IN THREE PLACES

Two Towns Captured Half Mile West Of Merzig

GENERAL Patton's Third Army troops have reached the River Saar at three places in the Merzig area. A one-mile front has been established along the river, cables Eric Downton, of Reuter's.

Russian Armies' Drive Continues

Last Ditch Bastion Of Nazi Defence In Hungary

BIG R.A.F. ATTACK ON DUISBURG

GAINS BY 8th ARMY IN ITALY

RUSSIA'S VITAL PART IN WORLD PEACE

Franco Will Be Told of Two Facts Irritating Britain

Air Chief for Middle East

Palestine Arrests Total 139

Christmas Nuts, 1lb per Family

BINNS MONTHLY HALF-PRICE REMNANT DAY

SOUTH SHIELDS
TEL. 1800.

217

CHAPTER 15

Delayed Deliverance: Life After Liberation

23rd April 1945 – Stalag IV-B, Mühlberg on Elbe, Germany

In the early hours, the German guards abandoned Stalag IV-B, stripped off their uniforms, donned civilian clothing, and tossed their weapons over the perimeter fence. The sound of distant artillery grew closer and by dawn, the tension in the camp was palpable. At 07:45, the first Russian troops arrived — Cossack cavalry men on horseback, followed by tanks, some driven by women. The red Soviet flag was hoisted and soon, flags of the other imprisoned nations joined it, fluttering in the morning breeze.

By 10:00, Russian and Serbian ex-prisoners marched out, free at last. Others, impatient to taste freedom, streamed into nearby villages, scavenging and looting supplies. Disease had taken hold in the overcrowded camp, exacerbated by poor sanitation and malnutrition. It took several days before order was restored.

On April 26th, a Russian Officer formally took command, placing the prisoners under Soviet control. Though technically free, the British and American prisoners were not immediately repatriated, and confusion reigned. Some refused to wait. It is estimated that around 4,000 men set off westward, alone, in hopes of reaching Allied lines — a dangerous journey through the chaos of a collapsing Germany. Russian patrols often turned back those they caught, while others vanished into the uncertainty of war-torn Europe.

Camp notices changed almost daily:

- "Evacuation will commence in a few days."
- "British and Russian staff officers expected in three days."
- "The whole camp should be evacuated by . . ."
- But no real movement came. Instead, the warnings grew more ominous:
- "Four men were returned by Russian patrols — solitary confinement."
- "Typhus spreading — those heading West are walking into danger."
- "No men are reaching the Americans — they're being intercepted by Russian forces and sent to other camps."

Despite these dangers, many men grew tired of waiting, including Albert, and after three weeks, he decided to take his fate into his own hands.

The Escape

Albert and his companions, including Charles Lindsay, his 101 Squadron crew mate, slipped out of the camp, unchallenged by the remaining sentries. Collecting their meagre possessions and whatever rations they had saved, they set off westward.

They walked for hours, covering more than 40 kilometres before reaching the banks of the River Mulde near Wurzen that evening. Exhausted but triumphant, they collapsed in a barn for the night, sharing space with other refugees, Russians and Germans alike, all caught in the shifting tides of war. They 'found' food along the way, and Albert was known to talk about having rustled piglets from a farmyard which they cooked and ate in the wild.

The next day, they walked towards Riesa, another 25 kilometres west. There, they found shelter in abandoned German officers' quarters, a step closer to home and, crucially, away from the barbed wire.

15.1   Freedom at Last – 20th May 1945

On 20th May, 1945, Albert and his fellow escapees reached the Mulde River Bridge near Bitterfeld. The bridge had been heavily damaged by bombing, with sections missing and the structure listing at a dangerous angle. Despite the risk, it was a crucial crossing point: beyond it lay the advancing American forces and safety.

A makeshift repair using wooden planks and a ladder bridged one of the gaps. Russian sentries were present but did not intervene, allowing the group to move forward.

Carefully navigating the unstable crossing, Albert, Lindsay and the others made it to the far side, where they were met by American soldiers. Firm handshakes and words of reassurance signalled the end of their long ordeal. Freedom was finally within reach.

That afternoon, they were loaded onto an American truck and driven 60 kilometres west to an aerodrome near Halle. Here, they found basic accommodation, safety, warmth, and regular meals for the first time in 16 months. Planes were departing almost daily, ferrying men onwards to Brussels. Now, it was only a matter of time to wait for their flight.

25th May 1945 – The Journey Home

Then the order finally came. It was met with urgency: "Three minutes to pack up and parade outside." They needed no more time than that. Within seconds, men had shouldered their meagre belongings and lined up, ready to go.

Outside, American twin-engine C-47 Dakota transport planes stood waiting, more than ten neatly lined up along the grassy edge of the landing strip. Affectionately nicknamed the "Gooney Bird," she earned this nickname because her large, lumbering image was likened to that of the giant albatross birds found on Midway Island in the Pacific. Despite the light-hearted name, the Gooney Bird was critical to undertaking support operations that helped win the war. She was capable of carrying 28 passengers at speeds of over two hundred miles per hour for long distances.

Albert clambered aboard with Lindsay. The once-familiar routine of flying now felt strange; for most, it was their first time in the air since the night they had been shot down. Five aircraft lifted off, one by one climbing into the sky. Below them, Germany shrank into the distance, hardship and worry now replaced with joy and hope. There was a sense of relief aboard the flight; the men laughed and joked. The war was over.

Two and a half hours later, their aircraft hit turbulence. It banked sharply, dropping into a sudden dive before levelling out. Moments later, they emerged from the clouds. Below lay an airfield, 30 kilometres south of Brussels, the historic site of Waterloo.

Touchdown was marked with a loud cheer. Once on the ground, the Red Cross greeted the weary men with tea, sandwiches, and cigarettes. They were taken by truck to a reception centre, where everything had been meticulously arranged. They signed identification papers and now the "dog tags" around their necks were no longer needed. Lindsay removed his and tucked them into his pocket, a keepsake of a dreadful chapter in his life. In short supply, fresh clothing and boots were allocated to those who were most in need; nobody escaped a thorough dusting down with delousing powder, which was administered to every nook and cranny!

Each man was given an accommodation assignment, where

they were treated to hot meals, warm showers, and fresh sheets. At a nearby Red Cross centre, they were provided with toiletries, chocolate, and cigarettes. They were also issued a small sum of Belgian francs, equivalent to five pounds, and a ten-shilling note for their arrival in England.

Belgian Francs issued to Albert.

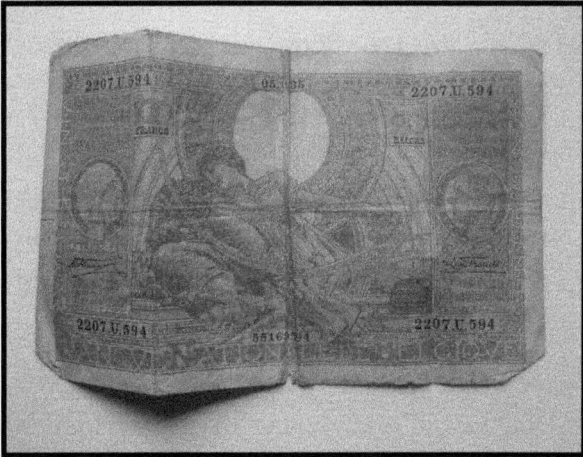

For the first time, they had the opportunity to wander through the city. That evening, Albert and Lindsay ventured into Brussels, marvelling at the sight of shop windows filled with goods, so different from the scarcity of the camp, though they quickly found that post-war Brussels was expensive.

15.2 The Last Barrier: McClure and Craig's Liberation

For Craig and McClure over in Stalag III-A, Luckenwalde, it was a similar situation.

The sounds of distant artillery grew louder each day, a sign that the Allies were closing in. Then, in April 1945, their liberation finally arrived.

Liberation by the Soviets – April 1945

On 22nd April, 1945, the camp gates of Stalag III-A were thrown open—not by their German captors, but by advancing Soviet forces. The Red Army had reached Luckenwalde, swiftly overpowering the last German resistance and setting the prisoners free.

The POWs, many too weak to celebrate properly, were suddenly faced with a new reality. They were no longer captives, but they were still stranded in a war zone. The Soviets, initially hailed as liberators, were reluctant to release British and American prisoners immediately. For weeks, confusion reigned as the Western Allies negotiated for their return. Eventually, arrangements were made and, by May 1945, most of the former prisoners were on their way home.

Another original piece of poignant poetry from the journal of James McClure.

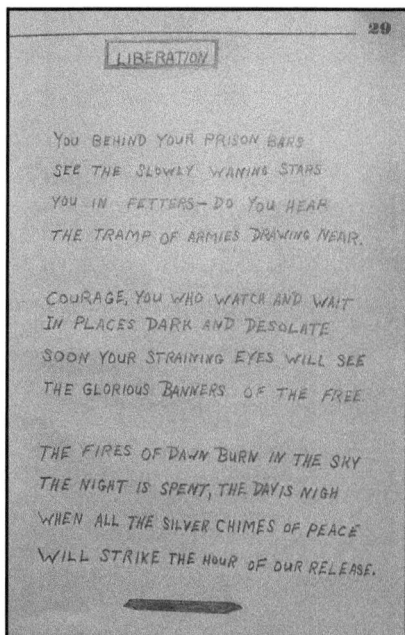

29

LIBERATION

YOU BEHIND YOUR PRISON BARS
SEE THE SLOWLY WANING STARS
YOU IN FETTERS – DO YOU HEAR
THE TRAMP OF ARMIES DRAWING NEAR.

COURAGE, YOU WHO WATCH AND WAIT
IN PLACES DARK AND DESOLATE
SOON YOUR STRAINING EYES WILL SEE
THE GLORIOUS BANNERS OF THE FREE

THE FIRES OF DAWN BURN IN THE SKY
THE NIGHT IS SPENT, THE DAY IS NIGH
WHEN ALL THE SILVER CHIMES OF PEACE
WILL STRIKE THE HOUR OF OUR RELEASE.

LIBERATION

You Behind Your Prison Bars
See The Slowly Waning Stars
You In Fetters – Do You Hear
The Tramp Of Armies Drawing Near.

Courage, You Who Watch And Wait
In Places Dark And Desolate
Soon Your Straining Eyes Will See
The Glorious Banners Of The Free.

The Fires Of Dawn Burn In The Sky
The Night Is Spent, The Day Is Nigh
When All The Silver Chimes Of Peace
Will Strike The Hour Of Our Release

For Weston Craig and James McClure, their ordeal as POWs had finally ended. The long road to recovery and rebuilding their lives awaited them—but they would carry the memories of those bitter winter months for the rest of their lives.

Many left with lifelong memories forged in captivity and a deep sense of camaraderie that only those who had endured the same horrors could truly understand. I wonder if many kept in touch.

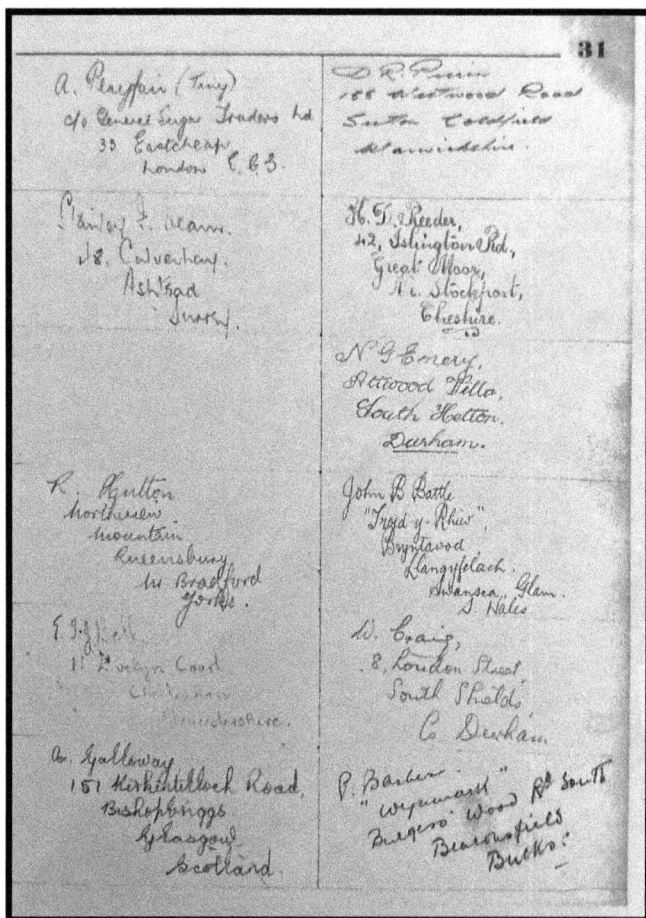

With immense gratitude to the family of Flight Officer James McClure, in particular daughters Brenda and Arlene and niece Cathy, for allowing us to share the sketches, records and poetry from the pages of his incredible journal.

CHAPTER 16

Operation Exodus: Coming Home at Last

Between 3rd April and 31st May, 1945, Operation Exodus facilitated the repatriation of thousands of liberated British prisoners of war. In total, approximately 354,000 men were flown home, many in modified Lancaster bombers. At the height of the operation, the repatriation aircraft were arriving in Europe at a rate of 16 per hour, bringing more than 1,000 people a day into British receiving camps. Albert's own unit, 101 Squadron, was among those tasked with this mission. The Lancasters were hastily modified, with their bomb bays stripped out to accommodate 24 ex-POWs seated along the fuselage in two rows. Any more passengers would have disrupted the delicate trim of the aircraft, making the journey dangerous. The aircrew was also reduced—from the standard team of seven to five men—since there was no longer any need for a bomb aimer or rear gunner. For the aircrew involved, the best times must have been when they could bring back one of their own.

In May alone, 15,088 men returned home using a variety of aircraft, including:

- 443 Avro Lancasters
- 103 Dakotas
- 51 Halifaxes
- 31 Liberators
- 3 Stirlings
- 3 Hudsons
- 2 Boeing B-17 Flying Fortresses

26th May 1945 - England at last

The following morning, Albert and his comrades were transported back to the airfield, where a Lancaster bomber awaited them.

Originally designed for warfare, these aircraft were not built for passenger comfort, but that was of little concern to the returning men.

As the Lancaster rumbled down the runway and lifted into the sky, a hush fell over the men. The drone of the engines was both familiar and strange, a reminder of what they had lost and a symbol of what they were about to regain. The aircraft climbed higher, leaving behind the ruined landscapes of war-torn Europe.

As they crossed the English Channel, thick clouds forced the plane into a sharp descent. When they finally broke through the cover, a new energy rippled through the men as the first glimpse of home was revealed by the striking white cliffs of Dover—a surreal and deeply moving sight that signalled they were nearing the safety of England. As the aircraft continued its journey, the scenery transformed into the lush green countryside of Oxfordshire, vibrant and welcoming, with small quintessential villages dotted along the way. Some men sat in stunned silence, eyes fixed on the landscape, as if afraid the vision might vanish; others erupted in cheers and claps, while a few wept quietly, over-whelmed by the immense relief of finally being home.

RAF Cosford and Recovery at 106 Personnel Reception Centre

Upon arrival in England in late May 1945, they were met with a hero's welcome and without delay each man was squirted down the front and back of the shirt and trousers with a pungent delousing solution—even the flight crew didn't escape! The hangars were adorned with flags and long tables were set with tea, served by members of the Women's Auxiliary Air Force (WAAF) and Auxiliary Territorial Service (ATS). Music played over the tannoy.

After a warm meal, the men were sorted by nationality and sent to reception camps. Albert was taken to 106 Personnel Reception Centre (PRC) at RAF Cosford, a hospital base in Shropshire, where he remained from 30th May to 4th June, 1945. Established in March 1945 as part of No. 24 Technical (Training) Command, No. 106 PRC served as a processing and recovery facility for liberated airmen, many of whom were in fragile physical and mental health. RAF Cosford's hospital provided medical treatment, rest and nourishment to help rebuild the strength of men who had endured years of malnutrition and hardship.

Jubilation was tainted with immense sorrow when Walton and Lindsay learned about the fates of their deceased crew members.

Albert, like many others, had changed profoundly. He was painfully thin, his uniform was tattered, and his body was weakened by months of poor nutrition and exhaustion. His spirit, however, remained determined and strong. Among his few possessions was a small bag of souvenirs—silk escape maps, a hidden compass, and scorched 100-franc notes. His sheepskin flying jacket, worn since his capture, had shielded him from the worst of the cold and remained one of his most treasured possessions.

Nearby airfields at RAF Seighford and RAF Wheaton Aston were used to ferry in former POWs. At Cosford, Albert underwent:

- Medical checks, confirming he was dangerously underweight (estimated at 8 stone).

- Processing of paperwork, including his POW Liberation Questionnaire, which recorded his time in captivity.

- Interviews with intelligence officers about his experiences in German camps.

- Reissue of uniform, identity papers, and back pay.

- Reintroduction to proper meals, though he, like many others, struggled to digest rich food after years of starvation rations.

To help them get back on their feet, the returning men were issued an advance payment and fresh uniforms. They were provided with a pamphlet containing information regarding the Reception Centre and a Welcome Message from the King.

But before they could fully return to civilian life, they had to go through intelligence debriefings. Every ex-POW was required to complete a Prisoner of War Liberation Questionnaire detailing their experiences. They were asked about German officers who had mistreated them, fellow prisoners who had collaborated with the enemy, and any escape attempts. Albert's own questionnaire, dated 27th May, 1945, records that while he was not mistreated, he was subjected to 14 days of solitary confinement and threatened with the Gestapo shortly after his capture.

After a few days of debriefing, medical treatment, and basic reconditioning, Albert was deemed well enough to return home.

Looking at the records, it's apparent that James McClure and Weston Craig had arrived back in England a week earlier than Walton and Lindsay.

Albert's POW Questionnaire

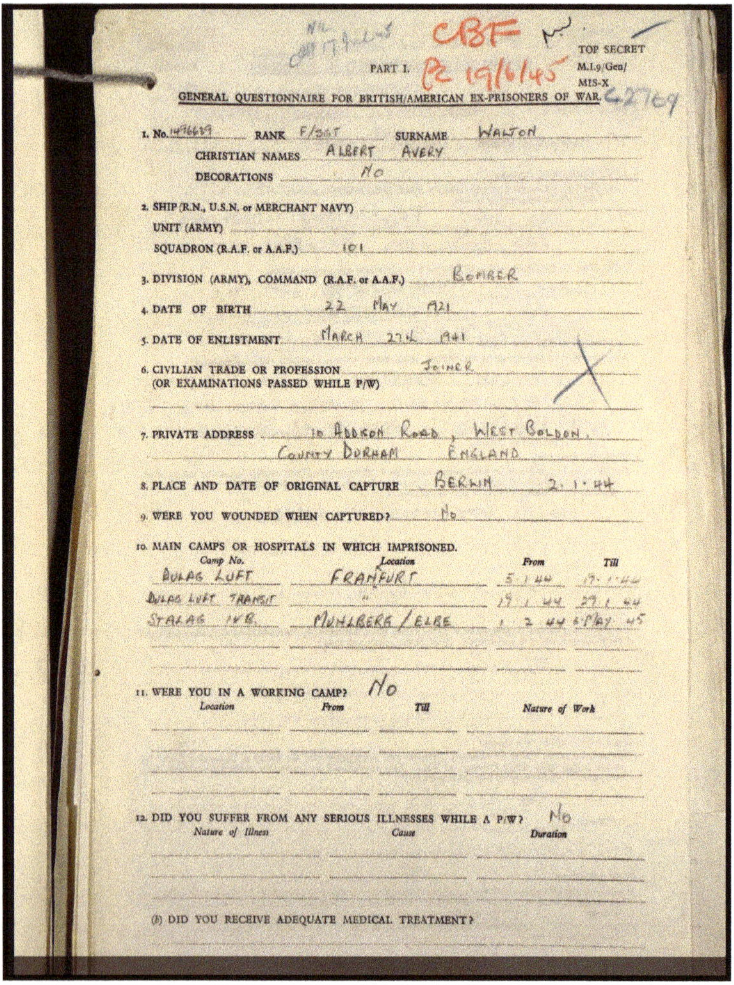

CBF
PC 19/6/45

PART I.

TOP SECRET
M.I.9/Gen/
MIS-X

GENERAL QUESTIONNAIRE FOR BRITISH/AMERICAN EX-PRISONERS OF WAR. 62769

1. No. 1476639 RANK F/SGT SURNAME WALTON

CHRISTIAN NAMES ALBERT AVERY

DECORATIONS NO

2. SHIP (R.N., U.S.N. or MERCHANT NAVY)

UNIT (ARMY)

SQUADRON (R.A.F. or A.A.F.) 101

3. DIVISION (ARMY), COMMAND (R.A.F. or A.A.F.) BOMBER

4. DATE OF BIRTH 22 MAY 1921

5. DATE OF ENLISTMENT MARCH 27th 1941

6. CIVILIAN TRADE OR PROFESSION JOINER
(OR EXAMINATIONS PASSED WHILE P/W)

7. PRIVATE ADDRESS 18 ADDISON ROAD, WEST BOLDON, COUNTY DURHAM ENGLAND

8. PLACE AND DATE OF ORIGINAL CAPTURE BERLIN 2.1.44

9. WERE YOU WOUNDED WHEN CAPTURED? NO

10. MAIN CAMPS OR HOSPITALS IN WHICH IMPRISONED.

Camp No.	Location	From	Till
DULAG LUFT	FRANKFURT	5.1.44	19.1.44
DULAG LUFT TRANSIT	"	19.1.44	29.1.44
STALAG IVB.	MUHLBERG/ELBE	1.2.44	6 MAY 45

11. WERE YOU IN A WORKING CAMP? NO

Location	From	Till	Nature of Work

12. DID YOU SUFFER FROM ANY SERIOUS ILLNESSES WHILE A P/W? NO

Nature of Illness	Cause	Duration

(b) DID YOU RECEIVE ADEQUATE MEDICAL TREATMENT?

1. No. 1496679   RANK F/SGT   SURNAME WALTON

CHRISTIAN NAMES ALBERT AVERY

2. LECTURES before Capture :
(a) Were you lectured in your unit on how to behave in the event of capture? YES
(State where, when and by whom).

CON. UNIT   FALDINGWORTH   SEPT 1943
RAF INTELLIGENCE OFFICERS

(b) Were you lectured on escape and evasion? (State where, when and by whom).

CON. UNIT   FALDINGWORTH   SEPT 1943
RAF INTELLIGENCE OFFICERS

3. INTERROGATION after capture :
Were you specially interrogated by the enemy? (State where, when and methods employed by enemy).

DULAG LUFT   FRANKFURT   5 MAY   19.1.44
SOLITARY CONFINEMENT 14 DAYS - BOGUS RED CROSS
FORM. THREATENED TO TREAT ME AS SABOTEUR AND HAND
ME TO GESTAPO

4. ESCAPES attempted :
Did you make any attempted or partly successful escapes? (Give details of each attempt separately, stating where, when, method employed, names of your companions, where and when recaptured and by whom. Were you physically fit? What happened to your companions?)

HAD NO CHANGE TO EVADE

5. SABOTAGE :
Did you do any sabotage or destruction of enemy factory plant, war material, communications, etc., when employed on working-parties or during escape? (Give details, places and dates.)

No

6. COLLABORATION with enemy :
Do you know of any British or American personnel who collaborated with the enemy or in any way helped the enemy against other Allied Prisoners of War? (Give details, names of person(s) concerned, camp(s), dates and nature of collaboration or help given to enemy).

No

7. WAR CRIMES :
If you have any information or evidence of bad treatment by the enemy to yourself or to others, or knowledge of any enemy violation of Geneva Convention you should ask for a copy of " Form Q " on which to make your statement.
(NOTE : Form Q is a separate form inviting information on " War Crimes " and describes the kinds of offences coming under this title.)

16.1 Operation Manna: Bomber Command and 101 Squadron's Humanitarian Mission

In the final days of World War II, 101 Squadron played a key role in Operation Manna, the first airborne humanitarian relief mission in history. Launched on 29th April, 1945, the operation aimed to deliver much-needed food supplies to the starving population of the Netherlands, which had suffered terribly under German occupation.

RAF Lancasters, including those from 101 Squadron, flew over designated drop zones across the country, releasing food parcels to the desperate Dutch people. In just ten days, nearly 7,000 tons of food were delivered, saving countless lives. By this stage, around 20,000 people had already died from starvation and almost a million more were severely malnourished, forced to survive on whatever they could find, including tulip bulbs and small animals.

The success of Operation Manna depended on delicate negotiations. A truce to be agreed between the Allies and Nazis had already begun in the winter of 1944/45, after pressure had been placed on Winston Churchill and President Roosevelt by Queen Wilhelmina and Prince Bernhard of the Netherlands, to ensure safe passage for the food drops. Air Commander Andrew Geddes, known to the Dutch as the Man of Manna, played a crucial role in organising the mission and securing the truce. Six air corridors were established, leading to designated drop zones such as Valkenburg Airfield, Rotterdam, and The Hague.

Despite the ceasefire, the mission was not without risk. Fearing a deception, the Germans stationed anti-aircraft units at some sites in case the aircraft carried paratroopers instead of aid. Some bombers even returned with bullet holes from rogue enemy fire. Tragically, three aircraft were lost—two in a mid-air collision and one due to engine failure.

Food packs, including tinned goods, dried supplies, tea, coffee, and chocolate, were carefully packed in hessian sacks to withstand the drops. The Dutch, who had only a day's notice, scrambled to collect and distribute the supplies. With first aid posts set up to deal with any injuries from falling parcels, thousands of lives were saved by this extraordinary mission, marking one of 101 Squadron's most remarkable contributions to history.

16.2 The Final Leg: Homeward Bound

With official clearance finally granted, Albert began the long-awaited journey north to Newcastle Central Station, the closest major rail hub to his home in Boldon. He boarded a crowded Edinburgh-bound train, his meagre collection of personal belongings in tow—among them, a bag of wartime souvenirs: scorched 100-franc notes, silk escape maps, and the small compass he had once hoped to use in an escape.

Seated beside him was Charles Lindsay, 'Jock', his comrade from 101 Squadron. The two men, having shared the extraordinary highs and lows of the last 18 months, were in good spirits, their excitement palpable. Conversations flowed easily between them, interspersed with laughter as they reminisced about their journey through war and captivity. Yet, beneath the surface, there was an unspoken understanding: this was their final journey together. The bond forged in hardship was now facing the inevitability of separation.

As the train rattled northward through familiar English landscapes, filled with returning servicemen, displaced families, and civilians rebuilding their lives, Albert felt the hours stretch into an eternity. The countryside rolled by, stations bustling with reunions, quiet faces staring out windows and, with each passing mile, anticipation built in his chest. This was the journey he had longed for, dreamed of, yet it carried an unexpected weight.

Back home in Boldon, his wife Lily and mother Caroline had scarcely slept, nerves and excitement intertwining as they prepared for the long-awaited reunion. Albert's earlier telegram: "ARRIVED SAFELY, SEE YOU SOON" had stirred both relief and impatience. His father, Alex, still suffered from injuries sustained in a wartime torpedo attack, and it remained uncertain whether he could make the journey to Newcastle. Regardless, for his family, years of anxiety and longing had culminated in this single day.

The final leg of the journey brought the train through York, Darlington, Durham, names that rang with familiarity. Then, the glint of the River Tyne appeared, and the sweeping arch of the Tyne Bridge came into view, a sight Albert had dreamed of countless nights behind barbed wire. His heart pounded as the train turned sharp left and slowed, wheels screeching, Newcastle Central Station drawing closer with every breath.

Yet, as the train came to a halt, a wave of conflicting emotions engulfed him. This was the moment he had awaited, yet now it meant saying goodbye. Albert turned to Lindsay. They shook hands, firm, lingering and exchanged a knowing glance. No words could capture what they had endured together, nor the gratitude they felt for having survived. A pat on the back, a fleeting smile. Then, Albert stepped down onto the platform, leaving his old life behind and stepping into a new world.

The stationmaster's whistle pierced the air. Doors slammed shut. The train, now bearing Lindsay further north towards Scotland, creaked into motion. Albert stood still and watched it pull away, his friend waving from the window until he was out of sight. His chest tightened, joy and sorrow intertwined. He had gained the warmth of home but left behind a brother-in-arms. It was, unmistakably, a bittersweet moment.

The Reunion

The platform was chaotic, families rushing, tears, laughter, the shouts of station guards. His eyes searched the crowd. His mother and Lily were there, but in the excitement of rushing forward, Caroline lost her footing and stumbled.

For a moment, everything else disappeared. The war, the prison camps, the hunger, the fear, it all faded into the background. Lily ran to him, throwing her arms around his thin frame. He felt so fragile, so light, his body weakened from the ordeal.

Caroline clutched his hand, looking him over with motherly concern.

"You're all skin and bones," she whispered, her voice thick with emotion.

Albert, once a strong and confident airman, now stood before them a shadow of his former self. He had survived, but the scars, both physical and emotional, would take time to heal. He now weighed just 8 stones, having lost one third of his body weight.

There was no fanfare, no parade, just a quiet, deeply personal and precious moment of reunion.

Recovery and a New Future

Albert was granted special ration cards to help him regain his lost weight. He spent weeks recovering at home, slowly adjusting to the reality of post-war life. The sudden freedom to relax, to eat, and to feel safe was almost overwhelming. The weight of the past few years hit him hard now that he finally had time to process everything.

16.3 Postman Delivers a Special Package for Albert

It took several years for war medals to be produced and distributed to Servicemen, the sheer volume required was enormous, running into millions. Albert was at home, having recovered from the physical and emotional toll of his POW ordeal, when the postman knocked at the front door. In his hands was a small but weighty brown package, stamped with the unmistakable 'Official Paid' postal mark. The moment Albert saw it, he knew exactly what was inside.

Inside the package were his well-earned war medals, a quiet but powerful acknowledgment of his service and sacrifice.

- The War Medal 1939–1945 – Awarded to British and Commonwealth forces who had served at least 28 days in full-time military service between 3rd September 1939 and 2nd September 1945.

- The Air Crew Europe Star – A prestigious campaign medal awarded to RAF aircrews who had participated in operational flights over Europe from bases in the UK.

- The 1939–1945 Star – A military campaign medal recognising service in the Second World War, first issued in July 1943.

As the medals were passed around, Caroline and Alex were immensely proud, especially when they read the accompanying letter from the Home Secretary. A ripple of excitement and admiration spread through the house. Yet, while his younger brothers and sisters looked on in curiosity, they couldn't fully grasp what these medals truly meant to Albert.

The Home Secretary presents his compliments and has the honour to transmit the enclosed Defence Medal which has been awarded in recognition of service during the war of 1939-45.

Ever the modest man, Albert never sought attention for his wartime experiences. He never wore his medals in public, nor did he speak much about his time in the RAF. To him, these medals weren't just decorations; they were a reminder of the comrades he had fought beside, the sacrifices made and the memories he carried in silence.

Albert's Medals

By July 1st,1945, he officially reported back for duty and was promoted to Warrant Officer. His survival, service, and resilience had been recognised.

But the road ahead was still uncertain. What did life after war look like? How would he move forward after everything he had endured?

For now, though, he was back on home soil and that was enough.

Albert's original Warrant Officer's badge
(hand embroidered)

CHAPTER 17

Life Depends on a Silken Thread

Like many of his colleagues in Bomber Command, Albert applied for Caterpillar Club Membership.

The history of the Caterpillar Club is as follows:

One evening in 1922, two airmen, Lieutenant Harold R. Harris and Lieutenant Frank B. Tyndal, met with parachute designer Leslie Irvin at McCook Field, near the site of what is now Wright-Patterson AFB USA. Over drinks, they shared stories of lives saved by parachutes and, from this conversation, the Caterpillar Club was born.

One of the airmen remarked:

"We ought to start a club for guys like us. As time goes by, more and more fliers all over the world will owe their lives to your chutes—it should be quite a thing in years to come."

The club's name symbolised the silkworm, whose thread was used to make the early parachutes. Its motto, "Life Depends on a Silken Thread," echoed the fragile yet life-saving nature of these devices.

Membership was exclusive: only those who had saved their lives by using an Irvin (IrvinGQ®) parachute from a stricken aircraft could apply. Both civilian and military personnel were eligible. Upon acceptance, members received an engraved gold caterpillar pin bearing their name, a membership card, and a certificate with their individual membership number.

Albert's Application to the Caterpillar Club

After returning to England from his time as a prisoner of war, Albert wasted no time in applying for membership to this elite club. The letter he wrote, dated 10th August 1945, survives to this day — a testament to the extraordinary events that led to his eligibility.

Original Letter Image

Image reproduced courtesy of IrvingGQ.

Letter Transcript

207 Charles St
10 Aug 1945
Boldon Colliery
Co. Durham

Dear Sir or Madam,

I wish to apply for membership in the Caterpillar Club. Returning from a raid on Berlin on the 16th of December 1943 all the members of our aircraft (Lancaster) had to bale out over England and again on the night of the 2nd of January 1944 we were hit by 'flak' over Berlin and had to abandon the aircraft by chutes. 4 of the crew were killed. I might add that the chute I used over Berlin opened in the aircraft and had two holes, one three foot and 18 inches in diameter, burnt in it – Even so I reached earth without injury. You will be able to get verification of these two jumps from my old Squadron – RAF Ludford Magnor, 101 Sqdn, Market Raisen, Lincs: The Pilot of the aircraft was F/LT. A. Lazenby. I remain Sir.

Yours Sincerely

1496639 W.O. Walton A.A.

Albert's Gold Pin, Membership Card and Certificate,
note promotion to W/O.

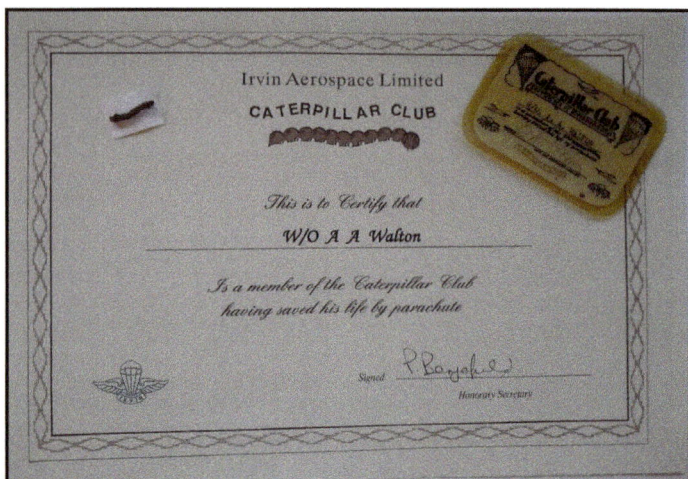

Throughout the rest of his life, whenever there was an occasion to wear a suit, Albert proudly pinned his golden caterpillar to his lapel. On the reverse was engraved: W/O A.A. Walton.

"A Badge of Honour!"

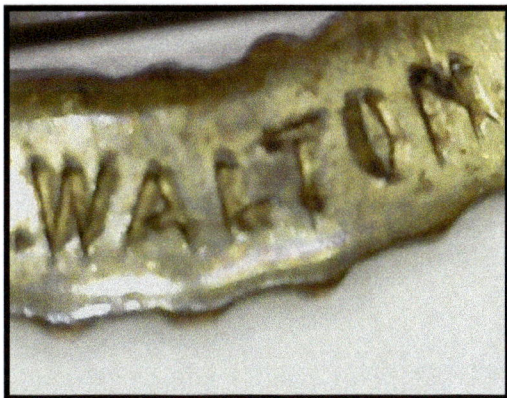

When we contacted Irvin Parachutes to inquire about whether they still held any records of our grandfather's membership, we were stunned to learn that they had retained his original handwritten application letter from August 1945.

Reading his words brought home the gravity of what he had endured. His parachute, the very device meant to save him, had accidentally deployed inside the aircraft and became burnt. Despite having two large holes in the fabric, it had carried him safely to the ground.

Only now do we fully appreciate what it means to be a member of The Caterpillar Club — a club that has been described as "the club that nobody wants to join." The experiences that led to Albert's membership were life-changing, marked by bravery, loss, and an unshakable will to survive.

And yet, in the end, all of that was symbolised by something so small and unassuming; a simple golden pin, shaped like a tiny caterpillar, worn quietly but with immense pride.

Crewmate McClure's Membership Card,
note promotion to F/LT.

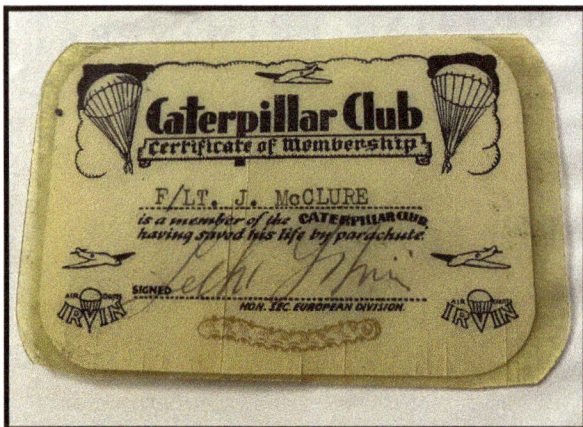

Lindsay's Caterpillar Club Membership and Gold Pin.

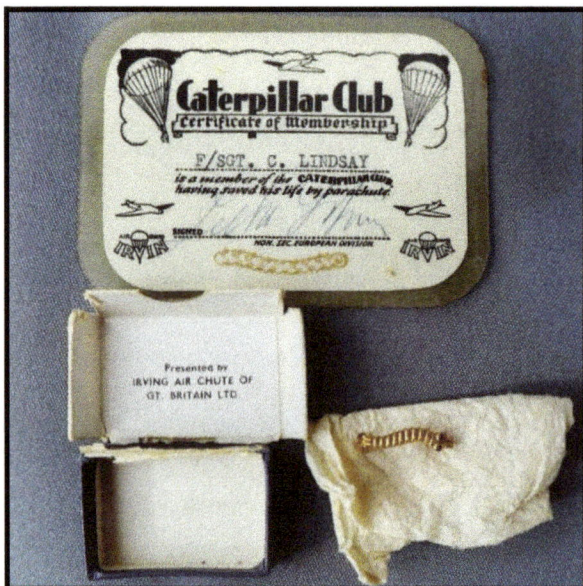

CHAPTER 18

Release from the RAF – The End of an Era

A fter more than five years of service, Albert Walton's time in the RAF came to an end in 1946. The war was over and, with it, the need for vast numbers of airmen. Like many others, Albert was gradually processed out of military life, making his way home to a country adjusting to peace.

His journey back to civilian life began on 27th March 1946. He travelled via RAF Scarborough, using a five-shilling travel voucher to cover the cost. Two days later, on 29th

March, he arrived at RAF Hednesford (104 P), a dispersal centre in the West Midlands. Here, airmen were formally classified for their release. Albert's dispersal class was P.O.W., reflecting his wartime experiences.

Although his official date of release was set for 9th June 1946, he was granted 72 days of paid leave, meaning his transition back to civilian life began immediately. Within his RAF Service and Release Book, Albert found various vouchers designed to ease the financial burden of returning home. A third-class travel pass ensured he could get back home without any out-of-pocket expenses, while a Medical Treatment Voucher provided reassurance that ex-servicemen would receive necessary care after years of war.

On 22nd July 1946, Albert cashed his final vouchers and collected his last military pay at Boldon Colliery Post Office. It marked the true end of his time in the Royal Air Force.

While one chapter of his life was closing, another was just beginning. The years ahead would be different: no more nights in briefing rooms, no more missions into the unknown. A new journey was just beginning; life as a father, husband, and civilian in a world forever changed by war.

18.1   Life Resumes in Boldon

With the war behind him, Albert embraced family life with open arms. In May 1946, he and Lily welcomed their first child, Kathleen, into the world. She quickly became the heart of their home, bringing immense joy and pride to her parents. The family lived in a small but happy home on Charles Street, Boldon Colliery, where they built a life filled with love and simple pleasures.

In the immediate aftermath of the war, Albert chose a quieter path, working on a farm in Boldon. The rural setting provided a sense of peace as he recovered physically, mentally, and emotionally from his wartime experiences. However, as time went on, he returned to a more active lifestyle, finding joy in work, sport, and community life.

Rationing and the Post-War Years

Rationing continued long after the war, even well into the 1950s. It affected everything, including wedding celebrations. When Doreen married John Tulip Walton (Albert's younger brother) in July 1950, the family had to pull together their resources.

Doreen recalls: "Uncle George, who worked at the Co-op in Yarm, was able to supply sugar, icing sugar, and eggs, allowing Sarah Ann to bake the wedding cake. It was a small but deeply cherished victory. A sign that life was finally returning to normal."

Albert and Lily's family grew over the years; their son Michael was born in 1948 and daughter Susan arrived in 1953. They were a brother and sister for their first child Kathleen, who arrived in 1946. By 1955, they had the opportunity to move into a brand-new council house on Hardie Drive. This modern home symbolised a fresh start.

Albert even had the chance to choose the house number off-plan, selecting number 101, a fitting tribute to his time in 101 Squadron.

Albert with children Kathleen (right), Michael (left), and Susan (middle)

Hardie Drive soon became a Walton family stronghold. Albert's sister, Elwyn and her husband, Jimmy, lived opposite 101. His parents, Caroline and Alec, settled further down the street, next door to Albert's brother John, his wife Doreen, and their family. His sister, Anne, and her husband, Leo, weren't far away, just a walk up the steep hill. The close-knit nature of the Waltons was well known and their gatherings were legendary. Whether it was seaside outings, countryside picnics, or fishing trips, they made the most of their time together, creating cherished memories.

Albert accompanied his younger sister, Anne, on her wedding day, walking her down the aisle. This was a great honour for Albert, he stood in for his father, Alex, who had ongoing mobility issues from his war wounds.

A Family That Lived for Adventure

Some of the most enjoyable aspects of being part of a big, lively family were the incredible days out that the Waltons planned and enjoyed together. Whether it was a trip to the beach, a countryside picnic, or a foraging adventure, these outings were about more than just fun: they were about creating memories, strengthening bonds, and celebrating the simple joys of life.

A 'Waltons' picnic (Albert and Lily on the left).

It wasn't unusual for a Walton family gathering to consist of twenty or more people. As soon as an idea for a day out was suggested, it quickly turned into a full-scale expedition. There was no such thing as just a small trip; everyone was invited and everyone came. It was a given that the Waltons did things big.

Seaside Days – Sun, Sand, and Soggy Sandwiches

A day at the beach was a military-style operation. Preparations would begin the night before, with food carefully packed into wicker picnic baskets, flasks filled with steaming hot tea, and tartan blankets rolled up and ready for use.

Early in the morning, the family would set off, often crammed into cars, vans, or whatever transport was available. If the journey was long, there would be a chorus of voices from the backseat: "Are we nearly there yet?"—a refrain that never failed to test the patience of the adults.

Once they arrived, there was no time to waste. The first task was to set up camp. Windbreaks were hammered into the sand, deck chairs unfolded, and towels spread out, creating a home away from home. The children, already in their swimsuits, dashed straight into the waves, shrieking as the icy North Sea sent shivers down their spines.

Lily, Albert and son Michael at the Seaside. Also pictured Stan Walton, seated with his son, John, and Doreen Walton along with Doreen's sister.

The adults, meanwhile, settled into their usual routines. The women laid out the picnic, shaking the sand from sandwiches that, no matter how carefully packed, always seemed to end up with a little extra 'crunch.' The men skimmed pebbles across the water or took a moment to simply sit back, breathe in the fresh sea air, and enjoy a well-earned rest.

The Waltons at South Shields Beach

For the children, the beach was a paradise. They built towering sandcastles, dug deep pits just to watch the tide fill them up, and played endless games of cricket or rounders. Some braved the waters for a swim, shivering, their lips turning blue as they insisted they weren't cold. Others searched rock pools for crabs, daring each other to pick them up before watching them scuttle back into hiding.

As the afternoon wore on, the beach would transform into a hive of different activities. Someone always had a kite and there was nothing more satisfying than watching it soar high above the dunes. At some point, there would be an impromptu wrestling match in the sand, usually ending in a fit of laughter as someone got buried up to their neck.

By late afternoon, it was time to pack up. Towels, now damp and coated in sand, were bundled into bags. The last remnants of the picnic were shared out, with arguments over who got the final piece of Lily's famous homemade fruitcake. Then, with the sun dipping lower in the sky, they would head home, tired but happy, the scent of salt and seaweed lingering in their hair.

Countryside Picnics – Nature's Playground

Beach trips weren't the only grand adventures. The Waltons also loved escaping to the countryside, where rolling green hills, bubbling streams, and hidden woodland clearings provided the perfect setting for a day of exploration.

Packing for a picnic was just as much a ritual as for the beach. Sandwiches, pork pies, and hard-boiled eggs were essential, as were bottles of homemade lemonade. A flask of tea for the adults was mandatory, along with a tin of biscuits for dunking.

One of the favourite countryside pastimes was tickling trout at Northumberland's River Wansbeck near Cambo, a skill passed down through generations. The children would crouch by the edge of a stream, hands submerged in the cool water, waiting for a fish to swim close enough to be gently 'tickled' before being scooped up. Whether they were ever successful was another matter, but the thrill of trying was entertainment in itself.

Wildflower picking was another favourite activity. The meadows and hedgerows were bursting with colour and as the family wandered through the fields, they gathered handfuls of daisies, buttercups, and bluebells. One particularly treasured memory was the annual tradition of picking wild daffodils in Northumberland, their golden heads swaying gently in the breeze as if welcoming their arrival.

At some point in the day, someone would inevitably produce a ball, and a game of football would break out. The adults joined in just as enthusiastically as the children, kicking up dust as they ran across the field, laughter echoing through the valley.

As the sun began to set, the picnic blankets were shaken out and the family sat together, watching the sky turn shades of pink and orange. These were the moments that mattered, the simple joys of food, family, and nature.

Blackberry Picking at Waldridge Fell – A Sticky Tradition

Autumn brought a new kind of adventure: the great blackberry picking excursions. Every year, the family would head to Waldridge Fell, baskets in hand, ready to gather as many jet-black berries as they could carry.

This was no casual outing; it was a full-scale harvesting mission. The best blackberries were always just out of reach, meaning the children would end up half-climbing, half-falling into the brambles, their hands and clothes stained deep purple. The grown-ups, slightly more patient, used walking sticks to pull down the highest branches, determined to collect the plumpest, juiciest berries.

By the end of the day, the baskets were full and the family returned home, exhausted but triumphant. The reward? Lily's famous blackberry jelly.

Unlike jam, which contained whole fruit, her jelly was silky smooth, made only from the strained juice of the berries. It was a labour of love, cooked down slowly, poured through muslin and left to set into deep ruby-red jars of pure sweetness. Slathered on fresh homemade bread or spooned over steaming hot porridge, it was the taste of autumn.

A Tight-Knit Community – Hardie Drive Life

Back home in Hardie Drive, life was just as rich and full as the family's countryside adventures. The neighbours weren't just people who lived next door; they were an extended family.

There was Mr. and Mrs. Simpson from across the street, always ready with a smile and a story. 'Auntie' Nancy and her brother, Albert Jenkins, felt more like real relatives than just neighbours. And then there was 'Auntie' Muriel, Mrs. Mathers, the Donnellys next door, and countless others who made up the fabric of this close-knit community.

The children of Hardie Drive grew up together, playing in the streets until the sun went down, dashing between houses where every door was open and every kitchen offered a snack or a friendly chat. In an era before television took over, evenings were spent swapping stories on front steps, sharing news over garden fences, and lending a hand whenever one was needed.

It was a time when neighbours truly looked out for one another. If someone was unwell, meals would appear at their doorstep. If a child scraped their knee, it wasn't just their mother who fussed over them; it was half the street.

Cherished Moments, Lasting Memories

Looking back, these were more than just days out or neighbourhood traditions. They were the heartbeat of the Walton family, a collection of moments, big and small, that shaped their lives and strengthened their bonds.

Whether it was windbreaks on the beach, picnic blankets in the fields, sticky blackberry-stained fingers, or late-night laughter on Hardie Drive, the Waltons knew how to make the most of life.

And at the centre of it all was family, a family that did everything together, loved fiercely, and made memories that would last a lifetime.

Albert's sister Hilda and some of the children visit Albert's brother John's allotment.

Life Down the Pit

Like many men in the area, Albert found work at Boldon Colliery, becoming part of the mining community that had long been the region's backbone. He took on the role of a Driftman, responsible for blasting new tunnels into the coal seams to prepare the way for the Hewers who mined the coal. It was a dangerous and highly skilled job, requiring expert knowledge of explosives and detonation techniques to ensure the tunnels opened in a controlled manner.

The work was physically demanding and fraught with hazards: flooded passages, collapsing ceilings, and unpredictable rock-falls were constant threats. Small pit ponies were often used to transport equipment through the narrowest of tunnels. On one occasion, a pony borrowed from a neighbouring mine was well cared for by the men, who regularly fed it crusts from their sandwiches and packets of Polo mints. After three months, when the job was complete, the miners discovered that their generosity had an unintended consequence: the pony had gained so much weight that it no longer fit into the cage to be brought back to the surface. It had to remain underground for several weeks on a strict diet before it could finally squeeze into the lift and return to its home.

Outside of work, Albert poured his energy into the things he loved most: gardening, football, and family. These passions defined his post-war years, shaping a life that, while ordinary on the surface, was rich with meaning and happiness.

Every now and then Albert would hold that little silver thrupenny bit tightly in his hand, remember his wartime experiences, and think how lucky he'd been to survive. He rarely mentioned his time during the war, a practice which seems to have been shared with his surviving crewmates.

Charles Lindsay's son, Kevin, recalled that his father rarely spoke about the war. However, one vivid memory surfaced from Christmas 1944 inside Stalag IV-B.

Kevin remembered a particular evening when, as a child in primary school, he eagerly performed Silent Night in German for his family, proud of his new linguistic skill. The reaction from his father was unexpected. Something in the song had stirred a memory long buried.

As the final notes faded, Charles quietly shared a rare glimpse into his past. As a POW, he had once heard the German guards singing that very same carol on a cold Christmas night behind the barbed wire. It was a moment of unexpected connection, an eerie reminder that, even in war, humanity could sometimes break through the barriers of captivity.

Albert similarly never spoke much of his ordeal. A quote from Jeff Walton, Albert's nephew, illustrates this:

"I spent a lot of time with Uncle Albert when I was young, say from about 8 years old to 13 years old. We went to all of Sunderland's home [football] games together and did lots of fishing on Sundays as well as lots of other family days out. As you can imagine, as a young boy I was very interested in what happened during the war, but other than being told he was shot down and taken prisoner, he always closed the conversation down and returned to talking about football." For him, perhaps, silence was the only way to manage the memories of that brutal time.

James McClure's daughter recalled, "My father never wanted to talk about his wartime experiences. As the eldest, I tried to understand what he had been through, but he would always refuse, simply saying, 'I don't want to talk about this now.'"

His younger daughter, Brenda, remembered how she and her sister were fascinated by their father's mysterious past in Germany during the war. As children, they longed to know more and, one day, they discovered his trunk filled with photos, sketches and wartime memorabilia. When he found out, he was reluctant to share details, closing the lid on those memories. It was as if that part of his life remained locked away, a chapter he wasn't prepared to reopen.

A relative who spent childhood holidays with Weston Craig's family was completely unaware that Weston ever served in the RAF, let alone that he had been a POW. It was a revelation that came as a total surprise, one he still struggles to fully comprehend. Weston had kept that chapter of his life so deeply buried that even those closest to him never knew the full extent of what he had endured.

CHAPTER 19

Back in the Game - The Football Years

Since his early days on the school football team, Albert's passion for the game never waned. After the war, he quickly resumed his playing career, this time as goalkeeper and captain, leading his team to victory in the local leagues. Albert played for the Bitulac team, alongside his younger brother John and brother-in-law, Leo Lloyd, whose contributions on the field were as vital as his own.

The Winning Team, 1952
(Below: Back (left to right): R. Bowen (secretary), A.
Walton (captain), A. Burden; centre (left to right): G.
Carter, J. Walton, A. Gilbert, J. Barnsley, Mr. M. Sawkill
(chairman); front (left to right): L. Lloyd, F. Lloyd, E.
Smith, E. Gibbons, S. Stephensen.)

Football was more than a sport for Albert; it was a way of life. When he wasn't actively playing, he could be found at Roker Park with his nephew Jeff, eagerly spectating, analysing tactics, and soaking in the atmosphere of match day. His enthusiasm extended to his family, who turned out in large numbers to support him at every game. His son Michael received an early taste of victory, as evidenced by a cherished photo of him proudly holding the championship cup, a moment that symbolised the joy and pride of the Walton family.

Albert front centre, son Michael also helping Daddy to hold the cup

For Albert, every match was a celebration of resilience and community, a reminder that even in the aftermath of war, life could still be filled with passion, teamwork, and triumph on the football pitch.

CHAPTER 20

Knowing Your Onions

It would be an understatement to say that Albert was a keen gardener. Even during his captivity in Stalag IV-B, he found solace in tending a small patch of earth behind the barbed wire. So, when he and Lily moved into their new home at 101 Hardie Drive, a house they certainly chose for its connection to 101 Squadron, it was no surprise that the garden quickly became his pride and joy.

At 101 Hardie Drive, Albert cultivated every inch of his modest front and back garden. There was no lawn, no patio, just rows of prize-winning giant leeks, onions, dahlias, and chrysanthemums. Four-foot-long carrots and parsnips were the norm. A greenhouse and deep leek trenches replaced any notion of a decorative garden. Lily didn't mind in the slightest; she knew how much it meant to him and encouraged him every step of the way. Besides, as a fantastic cook, she never wanted for a leek or an onion and Albert's produce made for the most delicious soup.

Albert with Prize Leeks

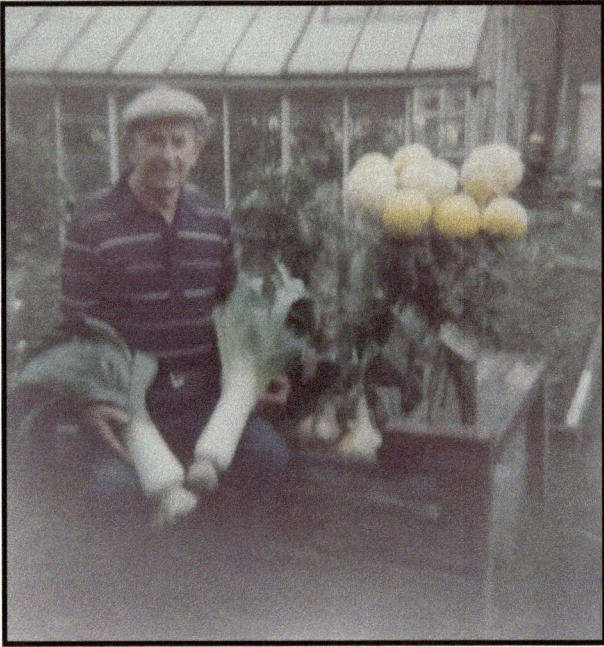

Great care went into mixing his secret soil formula, ensuring his crops reached their full potential. Even the rainwater barrels weren't just for collecting water; Albert made 'additions' to enrich the nutrients. Every sunny windowsill in the house was pressed into service for an early start to the growing season. Gardening came first and social occasions were often interrupted by his need to tend to the plants. One memorable example was a wedding reception in Boldon when a group of the men mysteriously disappeared for half an hour, only to be found at home, watering their leeks, because skipping a single day was simply unthinkable.

The greenhouse was Albert's sanctuary. Heated by an old green Valor paraffin stove to keep a constant temperature through winter, it was a place of peace, away from noise and distraction. Here, he could tend his precious tomato plants while enjoying a quiet Player's Navy Cut cigarette and a cup of tea. If anyone arrived unexpectedly, he would hastily stub out his cigarette, as if to hide the fact he'd indulged in the odd 'tab'!

As children, one of our jobs was to help with tomato pollination to increase crop yield. Armed with 'the tickling stick,' a long bamboo cane with a tuft of fur at the end, we would gently tickle the yellow flowers of the tomato plants, transferring pollen from one bloom to another. It was a vital task, taken very seriously.

Leek Shows and Fierce Rivalries

Leek and flower growing was a serious business in the Northeast of England throughout the 1960s, '70s, and '80s. Every social club hosted an annual flower show, where local men showcased their gigantic leeks and perfect flowers, while women competed with their homemade jams, fluffy Victoria sponges, and impeccably crimped pie crusts.

For Albert and his brother Stanley Walton, this was more than a hobby; it was a way of life. Gardening was in their blood and the annual competitions were the highlight of their year. But when it came to the shows, there was one unspoken rule: there were no shared secrets.

Sibling Rivalry at the Garden Shows

Albert and Stanley weren't just brothers; they were fierce competitors in one of the most prestigious local traditions, leek, vegetable, and flower growing. Albert was a dominant force at The Shack's show, where his carefully tended leeks, vibrant flowers, and flawless vegetables earned him countless trophies. His name was synonymous with success. But if Albert ruled The Shack, then brother Stanley was the undisputed champion at The British Legion show, just a stone's throw away. His reputation as a grower was just as formidable, and his collection of silverware proved it.

Naturally, with two brothers competing at the highest level, friendly rivalry was inevitable. Banter flew between them as they inspected each other's gardens, each looking for the slightest flaw in the other's produce. Albert would cast a critical eye over Stan's prized leeks and his gigantic blooms, while Stan would do the same in return. Neither ever revealed their growing secrets, but both would claim to know exactly how the other did it.

As show day approached, the competition intensified. Every year, their families and friends gathered to witness the battle unfold, quietly hoping that their man would take home the top prize. The brothers would support each other on their respective show days. When Albert won, Stan would give a reassuring nod of approval and a firm handshake. When Stan triumphed, Albert would shake his hand and feel very proud of his younger brother.

For the Walton brothers, victory didn't just come with a trophy; it came with soil-stained hands, a knowing smile, and the promise of another season ahead.

Brother Stan (on the right) being presented with the cup!

But despite the rivalry, there was always mutual respect. The Walton brothers were top growers and everyone in Boldon Colliery knew it.

The Shack's Leek Club

Albert was a founder member of The Shack's Leek Club, based in a social club near Boldon Pit — a popular gathering place for local coal miners. Every September, the annual flower show was a major event, demanding weeks of careful preparation.

Two weeks before the show, an official would visit each exhibitor's garden to stamp the flags (leaves) of the competition leeks, a measure designed to prevent cheating. Rivalries were intense and some men even stood guard over their leeks at night to deter sabotage.

In the days leading up to the event, Albert's garden became a hive of activity. Every prize vegetable had to be carefully excavated. The sides of deep wooden trenches were often removed to ensure that nothing was damaged during lifting, particularly the long, thread-like parsnip tails, which had to remain intact for judging.

Once lifted, the vegetables were taken indoors for a full-scale deep clean. This meant a long soak in the family bathtub, followed by meticulous scrubbing to remove every speck of soil. No one dared ask for a bath during this crucial process!

Show Day – The Moment of Truth

On the morning of the show, Albert was up before dawn, running on little sleep and agonising over every detail. His entries were arranged with military precision; each leek positioned for maximum impact, every flower petal checked for perfection. His 'Collection' display, one of the most coveted categories, was always presented on his lucky black velvet cloth, a tradition that had served him well.

The show hall was a sight to behold, tables laden with impressive displays of giant vegetables, dazzling flowers, and perfectly formed exhibits. The tension was palpable.

Once the doors closed, the judges deliberated in private for most of the day. The waiting was agony. By afternoon, the whole family would head to The Shack to see the results. Who had triumphed? Who would have to wait another year for their chance at glory?

Albert sweeping the board in 1989!

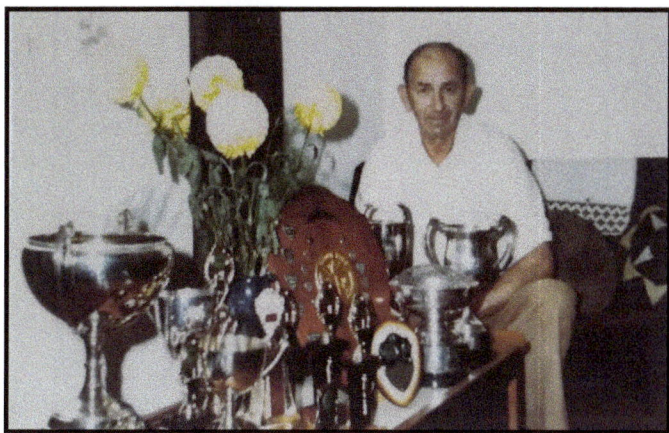

Albert and Lily went on to cherish one another for many years, their Golden Wedding anniversary being a major milestone. With the growing families of their own three children, nine grandchildren kept them busy and rewarded.

Photo taken on Golden Wedding anniversary. Albert is wearing his RAF tie

Albert's passion for growing never faded. He tended his beloved garden until the very end. He passed away one cold and frosty February morning in 1996, doing what he loved best — working the soil at 101 Hardie Drive.

His legacy was more than just trophies and ribbons. It was in the tradition, the hard work, the laughter-filled rivalry, and the simple joy of cultivating something from the earth.

Like Albert, the lives of his fellow 101 Squadron survivors went on to be full of rich memories and loving families.

20.1 Life After the War: The Journey of the Survivors

In the years following the war, the surviving members of our bomber crew each forged new paths in civilian life, carrying with them memories of camaraderie, sacrifice, and the bonds formed under fire.

Charles Lindsay returned to Carstairs, Lanarkshire, Scotland, where he resumed a clerical position within the railways. He eventually rose to the position of senior booking officer at Motherwell Train Station in Glasgow. He married his sweetheart, Jean, and together they built a family life, welcoming two sons, born in 1957 and 1958. They were devoted to one another and were exceptionally happy. Despite his post-war success and the warmth of family, Charles's life was cut short when he passed away in 1970 at the young age of 47. He left behind a legacy of hard work and quiet dignity.

Weston Craig initially returned to the Northeast of England and re-entered the civil service, a career that provided stability after the turbulence of war. In 1948, he married his beloved Daphne, and the couple moved around the south of England before finally settling in Cheltenham,

Gloucester. They raised two sons and a daughter, enjoying many happy years together. Weston's steady character and sense of duty remained with him until his passing in 1998. Remarkably, one of his grandchildren followed in his footsteps, becoming a Flight Lieutenant in the RAF, a fitting tribute to Weston's service and legacy.

James McClure made his way back to Winnipeg after the war. In 1948, he married Margaret and together they created a nurturing home. They were eventually blessed with two daughters, as well as grandchildren, nieces, and nephews. Employed for 43 years by the T. Eaton Company, McClure was also an avid sportsman who enjoyed bowling, hockey, fishing, and golf. He maintained ties with his wartime comrades through his active membership in the Pilots and Observers Association until his death in 1996.

Together, these men exemplified resilience, each carving out a new chapter in life while forever carrying the indelible memories of their wartime service. Their post-war journeys, marked by personal triumphs and quiet losses, remain a poignant reminder of the cost of war and the enduring strength of the human spirit.

The four comrades who perished as a result of the plane being shot down on the night of 3rd January 1944 will be commemorated forever in the Berlin War Cemetery

It has been an honour to record the adventures of our grandfather and his incredible life and family, from Boldon to Berlin and back again . . . along with the outstanding achievements of the men who were his family in the sky.

THE END

References and Acknowledgments

Written with heartfelt thanks to the following for their invaluable help, contributions and support:

Individuals and Families

Doreen Walton

Jeff Walton

Jill Stevenson

Julia, niece of Derek Brown and his brother Dave Brown

Anthony Freeman, relative of F/L Alan Lazenby

David Welch, relative of Weston Craig and Weston's family for their contributions to our book

Linda Grundy, relative of F/L Alan Lazenby

Duncan Woodward

Jennifer Macklin-Shaw, relative of Donald Stephens

Brian Walton

Helen Patton

Pauline Beadling

Anne Walton

Andrew Shepherd (Technical Support)

Joanne Chandler

Brenda Shaw, daughter of James McClure

Cathy McClure Niece of James McClure

Arlene Solvason daughter of James McClure

Kevin Lindsay, son of Charles Lindsay

Tony Noble
Triinu Metts
Chris Anderson
Neil Walton
Damian Storey from DLS Automobilia and Militaria
Gerald Britton relative of Gerald Beckett
Neville Chamberlain

Groups and Organisations

101 Squadron Association Paul Thompson
101 Squadron Association Gary Wright
RAF Bomber Command Forum
Ministry of Defence
Caterpillar Club
Tennants Auctioneers
Boldon History Facebook Group
Boldon FC

Archives and Contributors

Malcolm Ramsay at CASPIR – Gerald Beckett photo
Erica, Imperial War Museums – FIDO photo
Paul Johnson, National Archives – Flight Log Information
The British Newspaper Archive
IBCC – Dr Dan Ellin, Archivist
This project would not have been possible without your insights, memories, photographs, encouragement, and dedication to preserving history.

www.ingramcontent.com/pod-product-compliance
Ingram Content Group UK Ltd.
Pitfield, Milton Keynes, MK11 3LW, UK
UKHW050349140925
462858UK00001B/1